Haunted Travels
of
Michigan

Haunted Travels
of
Michigan

Kathleen Tedsen & Beverlee Rydel

Thunder Bay Press

Holt, Michigan

A BOOK & WEB
INTERACTIVE EXPERIENCE

www.hauntedtravelsMVG.com

Haunted Travels of Michigan
by Kathleen Tedsen & Beverlee Rydel

Copyright © 2008
TR Desktop Publishing

All Rights Reserved

Published by
Thunder Bay Press
Holt, Michigan 48842

First Printing July 2008

15 14 13 12 11 10 09   10 9 8 7 6 5 4 3 2

ISBN: 978-1-933272-18-4

All photos taken by the authors except where credited.
Book and Cover design by Julie Taylor.
Back cover image courtesy of Metro Paranormal Investigations.

Printed in the United States of America
by McNaughton & Gunn, Inc.

Contents

Preface

These stories have been written in the first person to bring the reader into an investigation on a more personal level. Each story, however, has been a joint writing effort between the authors.

As writers of the *Michigan Vacation Guide: Cottages, Chalets, Condos, B&B's* book series, we have visited hundreds of lodgings and numerous restaurants, pubs, and historical sites across our state. Over the past sixteen years, we have met many reputable people who have experienced something so powerful they have become true believers in the paranormal. These individuals have told us fascinating stories and identified locations they sincerely believe to be haunted. Are they simply ghost stories, urban legends, and folklore, or are they fact? That's what we'll be investigating.

We want to go beyond the ghost stories and urban legends. We want to take you with us on our journey into some of Michigan's most reputed haunted bed and breakfasts, inns, hotels, restaurants, and other well-known locations as we investigate the unknown. We want you to see what we see, hear what we hear, feel what we feel.

Join some of Michigan's most reputable paranormal groups as they conduct investigations. Enter the stories and history of each location as we reveal the haunted facts… with a skeptic's eye.

Our experiences will sometimes be funny, sometimes thought-provoking, and sometimes chilling. The stories and evidence revealed in this book and Web site will be true, unaltered, and accurate. You'll see it and hear it just as we did (audio adjustments may be made for clarity). Ultimately, whether or not a location is haunted will be your decision.

Enjoy this book by itself, or join us online for a complete interactive book/Web experience. You will be able to hear the electronic voice phenomenon (EVP), see up-close the unusual photographic and video evidence, listen to behind-the-scene activities and interviews, and more as you follow along in the book. Our journey into the unknown is just beginning… come with us.

Story Secret Rooms

How to Use Our Interactive Web site
www.HauntedTravelsMI.com

To help bring you into each story, we have established a Web site, www.HauntedTravelsMI.com, with a "Secret Room" for each story. This Secret Room will include audio, video, and full color photographic evidence. It will also have some behind-the-scene video clips and/or photographs of what happened during the investigation.

Secret Rooms are Password Protected

Each story has a secret password that will unlock the room. You must enter a separate password for each Secret Room.

High Speed Internet Recommended

Because the file size for some videos, photos, and audio clips are large, for best results, you should have a broadband or high speed Internet connection. You can use dial-up, but you'll need patience.

How It Works

Step One: Go to our Web site: www. HauntedTravelsMI.com and click on "Secret Rooms." This will get you to the doorway to enter the Main Secret Room Vault. You'll see a wooden door. *CLICK ON THE DOOR HANDLE.*

Step Two: You are now in the Main Secret Room. Click on the number associated with the story, (example: The Whitney Restaurant is Story #1).

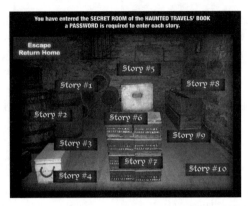

Step Three: Once you click on the number, a dialogue box will come up saying you're about to enter a password protected page. *CLICK OK.*

Step Four: The Password box will come up. Carefully *ENTER THE PASSWORD* from the story, then *CLICK OK.*

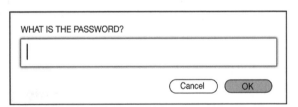

Step Five: Another dialogue box will come up. If you've entered the password correctly, it will let you know. *CLICK OK.* If you've entered the wrong password, it will re-direct you back to our main page. You'll need to try again.

That's it!
You've unlocked the Story Secret Room door.
Your virtual experience begins.

Story One
The Whitney Restaurant

Whitney Restaurant, exterior made of jasper granite

Detroit, Michigan
Web site: www.HauntedTravelsMI.com
Secret Room Password: wr73d
Paranormal Investigative Team:
Highland Ghost Hunters

The Whitney, one of Detroit's most prominent five-star restaurants, has been serving guests since the 1980s. Built in 1894, it was once the private residence of Detroit's wealthiest citizen, David Whitney Jr.

This twenty-one thousand square foot mansion features fifty-two rooms, twenty fireplaces, and a secret vault. It is elegantly designed with sweeping staircases, Tiffany lamps, intricately detailed wood, beautiful stained glass, and imported marble. The exterior is made from hardy jasper granite giving the home its unique pink hue.

Dining at The Whitney is truly a unique event. Intimate dining rooms make your visit a personal experience. Of course, there are larger rooms for catered events. The restaurant's award-winning chefs have perfected the art of refined dining. Add to that an award-winning wine cellar, and you have an unforgettable evening. The Whitney is just down the road from Detroit's theatre and entertainment district, making the restaurant and its third floor lounge a great spot either before or after a night out on the town.

Grand staircase shows the home's impressive workmanship

Intimate dining rooms

Tales of The Whitney's haunting began with the home's transition to a restaurant. In fact, a December 1986 article in the *Detroit Free Press*, "The Whitney, an American Palace" mentions an unusual event. In late October, as final renovations were nearly complete, a mysterious fire started in two bedrooms. The cause of the fire was questionable but, according to the article, may have begun with "…spontaneous combustion of cleaning rags…"

Some people in the paranormal community believe that renovations can create higher levels of spiritual activity. If the energy that exists is not pleased with the renovation, it may respond in a negative fashion. Of course, it's impossible to say that the mysterious "spontaneous combustion" fire was a negative response by spirits, but it was a curious event.

Since that time, there have been frequent reports of unusual phenomena. The most often reported are mysterious shadows, apparitions, voices, and the well-known *haunted elevator*. This elevator seems to have a mind of its own, traveling from floor to floor transporting its unseen guests.

Our first experience at The Whitney was back in 2005. After enjoying a sumptuous dinner, we explored this amazing home.

We took a few casual photographs and brought an audio recorder just for fun. What we captured was unexpected and, to date, defies explanation.

The first was a photograph taken by the elevator. Bev was alone at the time when she took the picture on the second floor. It is a very clear photo of the elevator and hallway. A rather unremarkable photo if it were not for a strange anomaly in the lower left corner. It is in this area an unusual tunnel-shaped mist or vortex appears. Formed almost like a little swirling tornado, the

Elevator with vortex

very top appears to have an eye in its center. This anomaly is coming from the elevator and shows movement past a wastebasket. Some believe a vortex is an opening to the other side. Could this be what the photo captured?

We also recorded two EVPs. These were captured when I was with a small group of people on the second floor. We were in what used to be Mrs. Whitney's bedroom. Voices can be clearly heard in-between a conversation. The whispered

Vortex enlarged

voice first says, "Get out." Then, a second or two later, "Get out now." The color photo and EVPs can be heard in this story's Secret Room.

When Jenny and Lisa, co-founders of Highland Ghost Hunters, contacted us to join them on an investigation of The Whitney, we

Lisa Mann and Jennifer Marcus, Founders Highland Ghost Hunters

jumped at the opportunity. A few weeks before joining Highland, we began to research the home and its influential family.

The elegance found in this home was rare in 1900 America and was seen only in the residences of our country's most elite citizens. That would certainly apply to David Whitney Jr.

In 1857 David Whitney Jr. left Massachusetts to head up the Detroit division of his lumber company. A shrewd businessman, he began to purchase woodlands in Michigan and surrounding states. By the 1870s David was one of the Midwest's largest lumber barons. He soon owned a fleet of Great Lakes ships and was heavily involved in banking and other Detroit businesses.

On one of his travels to Canada, he met and eventually married Flora McLaughlin. Flora was said to be kind, very patient, and to have a wonderful sense of humor and an enormous capacity for love.

As Mr. Whitney's wealth grew so did their family. Their first child was Grace. David C. was next, followed by Flora Ann and Katherine. Though they grew up in a privileged, idyllic life, they showed an amazing compassion for people in need.

Sadly, Mrs. Whitney's heart was not strong, and in February 1882, she passed away. This was an incredibly difficult time for David who, by all accounts, was devoted to her. That is why we were somewhat shocked to learn Mr. Whitney remarried just a

David Whitney Jr., one of early
Detroit's wealthiest men

Flora Whitney, David's first wife

year and one month after Flora's death, in March 1883. Perhaps even more curious was whom he married. It was Flora's younger sister, Sarah. Sarah McLaughlin lived with the Whitney family for a few years before Flora's death.

We suspect the marriage was more of convenience than romantic love. At the time of the marriage, Sarah was thirty-eight years old and unmarried. In that period, a woman relied completely on her husband's income to survive. Adding to the likelihood of a marriage of convenience is the fact that Sarah's bedroom was on the second floor and Mr. Whitney's on the third floor. Though it was common for husbands and wives to share separate bedrooms in this era, it was uncommon for the bedrooms to be on different floors. It seems most likely that Mr. Whitney married Sarah as a kind gesture to ensure she was provided for after his death.

Both David Whitney and Sarah Whitney died in the home. David passed away November 28, 1900 after a two-week illness. Sarah died seventeen years later. During their illness, the elevator was in constant use transporting physicians, nurses, and family members. The elevator was eventually used to transport their bodies to the coroner.

As our research continued, we learned that Mr. Whitney was a quiet, dignified man who did not flaunt his wealth and avoided unpleasant situations. He was also a devoted father and would do almost anything for his children.

Perhaps closest to his heart was his oldest daughter, Grace. Just like her mother, Grace had a wonderful sense of humor and cared deeply for the welfare of others. When Flora died, Grace took over care of the Whitney household and even helped her father with some of his business dealings.

Grace Whitney

Both Grace and Katherine were accomplished pianists. It was not unusual for Mr. Whitney to come home after a busy, stressful day and ask one of his girls to play. Music, in fact, was a big part of the Whitney family. They frequently attended and presented recitals with music from the great composers. Ludwig Von Beethoven's "Moonlight Sonata" was among their favorites.

Katherine Whitney

Reprinted from *Grace Whitney Huff: The Story of an Abundant Life*, by Carolyn Patch, 1933

Photograph courtesy of the Whitney family

Not long after graduating from high school, Grace Whitney met and married a sweet young man by the name of John Everett Evans. As a wedding gift, Mr. Whitney gave the newlyweds his former home on Brush Street, not far from the magnificent

Whitney mansion. They had one child together, Elaine. She was particularly pampered and spoiled by the entire Whitney family. Sadly, Grace's husband died just eight years after the marriage. From that point on, Grace became heavily involved in charitable works and was known for her selfless efforts to help those in need.

Several years after John's death, Grace journeyed to France. There she met and fell in love with, literally, an American in Paris. His name was John Hoff. John was an American citizen sent to France to head up Standard Oil's European operations. Around 1883, John and Grace became engaged. Though Grace deeply loved John, the marriage would pose a problem because it would require she move to Paris. She asked John to keep their engagement secret until she could find the right moment to tell her father. What Grace did not know is that her younger sister Flora Ann was about to make an announcement that would throw the entire family in turmoil and keep Grace's engagement secret for several years.

Apparently, young Flora Ann met and fell in love with a worldly Swiss philanthropist named Rudolph Demme. Mr. Whitney, having a strong antipathy for foreigners, adamantly opposed this marriage. He was also distraught that his daughter would move so far away and secretly feared Rudolph would hurt her. He and Flora Ann argued vehemently. Emotions ran high. Just before the marriage, Mr. Whitney vowed to disinherit her. This announcement made headlines in major U.S. newspapers, including the *New York Times*. Despite the threat, Flora Ann married Rudolph in June of 1895.

Try as we might, we were not able to discover what happened between father and daughter after the marriage. It is unknown if Mr. Whitney actually disinherited Flora Ann or if they ever made up before his death. It does appear, however, that Mr. Whitney's fears were quite accurate. An article in the *New York Times* dated September 27, 1906 stated that Flora had divorced Rudolph, "… his conduct in Italy led to a sensational separation and divorce." Little is known about his scandalous conduct in Italy, but we can imagine.

At the time Flora Ann announced her marriage plans, Grace tried to keep peace within the family. She continued to keep her own engagement secret. Shortly before Flora Ann and Rudolph's marriage, Mr. Whitney's health began to decline. Grace continued to hold back the announcement of her engagement, fearing the news would be too much for her father to bear. Finally realizing she and John could wait no longer, Grace decided to break the news.

Wanting to say exactly the right words, Grace wrote a lengthy letter and gave it to Mr. Whitney's secretary. Grace told her to give it to Mr. Whitney on a day when his health was good. She also asked the secretary to immediately call her when Mr. Whitney was given the letter and she would come.

Several days later, Grace received a call. The letter had been given to Mr. Whitney. When Grace entered his office, she found him with the open letter and his head bent over the desk. One of his associates, General Alger, came into the room. Mr. Whitney looked up and sadly said to the General, "My daughter is going to leave us."

Grace's wedding was held in the Whitney mansion. It was a grand event that was well attended. Later that afternoon, the Whitneys brought Grace and John to the train depot. Before leaving, Mr. Whitney said to John, "You have taken my greatest treasures. Care for them." As the train left the station, Grace looked out to her father. He smiled and waved but there were tears in his eyes.

This would be the last time Grace would see her father alive. Just a few months after their arrival in France, Grace received a telegram that he had become seriously ill. She and John took the next ship back to America. Unfortunately, by the time they arrived Mr. Whitney had passed away. Grace was devastated. During the next several days, she would sit down at the piano and play their favorite pieces. She said that if her father could not see her, he would most certainly hear her play and know that she was there.

It was a fascinating story of the Whitneys as well as a touching and sad end to an amazing life. The research was intense and difficult, but we were happy to have a more complete picture of the Whitneys and what had transpired within the home. We were ready for the investigation.

We met Jenny, Lisa, and their team in the Whitney parking lot on an unusually warm October evening. Jenny and Lisa briefly assembled the group to go over their plans for the investigation. As the guests began to leave, we went inside to meet with Kristine, the manager.

Kristine Rader (far right), Dining Room Manager talks about the haunting

She began by giving us a tour of the main building, pointing out the key areas of paranormal activity. The most active areas in restaurant were on the second and third floor. In particular, the second floor Ladies' Room, as well as the rooms that were once Mr. and Mrs. Whitney's bedroom on the second and third floor. Several employees had also reported seeing the apparition of Mr. Whitney on the staircase.

Kristine recounted one personal experience she had on the second floor. She was alone putting up holiday decorations late one evening. From the corner of her eye, she kept seeing shadows. This went on for some time, and with every shadow she became more anxious. It reached a point that she finally had to leave because she was just too frightened to stay.

Kristine also talked about the crazy elevator. Since the first opening of the restaurant in 1986, the elevator has mysteriously moved between floors. She also told us about a servant dressed in formal attire that is often seen in the Whitney's private dining room. The sound of dishes being stacked is also a common phenomenon.

Finally, she led us out to the old carriage house. This building, next to the main house, was formerly used as the Whitney's horse

Carriage House

stable. Now, it is primarily used for storage. Unlike the home, the carriage house has not seen recent renovation. The horse stalls still remain on the first floor but are filled with miscellaneous clutter. It was dark and intimidating as we ascended to the top floor. The group carefully avoided dead birds and other debris on the way up. Obviously, it had been awhile since anyone had traveled this area.

The third floor was void of light except for a small window that shed a faint glow into the room. It was musty and filled with dead air. An eerie hush suddenly fell on the group. There, in the middle of this bleak, dirty room, was a perfectly set table for two. Table Number 25. A layer of dust covered the elegant linens, china, stemware, and silver. It was a setting that seemed to beckon two lost lovers for a romantic rendezvous.

Table 25 still waiting for its party to arrive

As we stared at the setting, Kristine whispered, "It's been up here for a while." She continued, "No one had been here for years until a member of the staff came up to store some things. There it was. We have no idea when it was set or why. No one has the heart to touch it since it was found. We don't know. Perhaps one day the guests will arrive."

With that, the tour was over. Kristine led us to the main house where we would begin the formal investigation after a short break. What we did not know, what we could not anticipate, is that we were about to investigate one of our most haunted locations.

Team sets up

By 2:00 A.M. the building was empty and HGH began equipment setup. Audio, video, EMF, and thermo gauge equipment, though checked before the investigation, were re-checked one final time. Jenny took EMF base readings throughout the building to record normal room levels. This would help identify unusual EMF spikes

Jenny takes base readings

as the investigation progressed. Meanwhile, Lisa and the team began positioning independent video cameras at key locations. Cameras were anchored in front of the second floor staircase and elevator. Also, each group would have at least one hand-

Lisa and Curt discuss equipment positions

held video camera and
several still cameras.
Audio recorders were
carried by members and
also placed throughout
the building. We were
soon ready to go dark.

Maria, HGH sensitive,
led the group in a cleansing prayer

Everyone gathered
for a cleansing prayer.
After that, we were ready
to go. Jenny and Lisa gave
a last-minute reminder
to not whisper or walk
during EVP sessions
to avoid evidence
contamination. With
that, the group divided
into two teams. Lisa's
team headed to the third
floor while Jenny's team
remained on the second.
Each would hold their
positions for about an
hour.

Room temperature and EMF
readings are taken

Around 2:30 A.M. Jenny was doing a second EMF sweep when
a sound was heard. "What was that?" she said. "Is that dishes?"

My response, "I heard it too."

Indeed, the faint but familiar clanking of dishes had been heard.
Believing the sound came from the first floor, our team quickly
moved downstairs. We scanned the various rooms. There was no
one around. Nothing was disturbed in the kitchen. We headed
down the hallway in time to hear a soft whir, like a motor. The
elevator doors opened. Empty. They quickly closed, taking their
unseen visitor to another floor.

During this time, Lisa's group was stationed in a third floor back
room. Curt was taking temperature readings. Holding the gauge

steady, he targeted the center of the room. The temperature remained fixed at 66 degrees. Then he noted sudden fluctuations beginning to occur. There was a rapid drop from 66 degrees to 57 degrees. Within the span of a few minutes, the temperature had dropped, the sound of dishes was heard, and the elevator doors had opened.

Temperature drops to 66, eventually going down to 57

Everyone regrouped around 3:00 A.M. for a short break. Once outside, we spoke with Kristine and the bartender. Both confirmed they had not gone into the restaurant for any reason over the past hour or two. So the cause of dishes being rattled still remained unanswered. With the break over, both teams headed to their new locations. Lisa's group went to the second floor and Jenny's to the carriage house.

Elevator doors open

Up to this point, the team's sensitive, Maria, had remained relatively silent. The atmosphere changed, however, as Maria entered the third floor of the carriage house. "It's less friendly here... a little darker," she murmured.

She sensed an unsettling energy and continued, "If it decides to make its presence known, I think we should leave it at that. I don't think I want to do too much to invite trouble, because I don't think any of us want to take that home. If it decides to attach itself to you, you have problems."

It was then I caught a movement on the floor and swung my video camera downward. My lens captured an enormous roach darting rapidly from where Maria and I stood. It is said that roaches are a sign of paranormal activity. Everyone became alert, especially Jenny, who just happened to be wearing open-toed sandals. Our anticipation was greeted with silence.

Meanwhile, Lisa's team was quietly doing EVP work on the second floor of the restaurant. In one of the bedrooms, the group was asking Mr. and Mrs. Whitney questions. Curt was again monitoring temperature. The gauge read a steady 70 degrees. Challenging any spirits in the room, he asked them to drop the temperature to 62 degrees. Within moments, he noted a steady decline until it reached exactly 62 degrees. He asked for the temperature to drop lower. It did, heading down to 57 degrees before slowing moving back to its previous 70 degrees. They threw out the same challenge ten minutes later, but this time the temperature remained steady. There was no further response.

Around 4:00 A.M. the investigation concluded and equipment was being disassembled. Bev was on the second floor doing a final walk-through along with Sean and John from HGH. Bev went into a back room. The elevator, which had remained silent for some time, unexpectedly opened. Sean and John turned and watched. It was 4:15 A.M. Bev returned and the two men told her the elevator was beginning to act up again. The threesome waited for a few minutes, watching the doors in anticipation. When nothing further happened, Sean and John decided to go upstairs to help Lisa and Curt finish packing equipment.

Bev remained on the second floor taking photographs. Finally, about ready to leave, she called for a final response. "This is your last chance. If there is anything you want to say, do it now because we're getting ready to leave."

A pause, then she continued, "I'm going down to the first floor." With that, Bev picked up her camera gear and left. The stationary video camera recorded her leaving and the sound of her retreating

Second floor where Bev asked her last EVP question

footsteps. She paused briefly on the staircase before continuing to the first floor.

It was almost daybreak when everyone regrouped on the first floor. Though exhausted, we all felt a sense of satisfaction. It had been an interesting hunt, but at that time, we had no idea how eventful it had really been.

After a well-needed rest, our love-hate relationship with evidence review began. Reviewing hours and hours of video and audio is a time consuming, tedious process. It is, however, one of the most important parts of any investigation.

Evidence review in this investigation would be a little different for us. HGH had turned over copies of all their audio and video. Both teams could now conduct independent reviews. Of course, Bev and I always go over our material but rarely have the opportunity to examine material collected by the paranormal teams. It would mean a few extra days of evidence review, but it was nothing compared to the long days HGH would spend on analysis.

After going through hours of video and audio, we were ready to give it a wrap. Between the HGH team, Bev, and I, we had collected a few interesting audio clips with EVPs but nothing noteworthy on video.

Then we popped in the final DVD that represented the last two hours of the investigation. We were pretty much lulled into a state of numbness when the first event happened. It was brief. Like the blink of an eye. Nothing that startling but it caught our attention.

Several minutes passed. Then one of the most unsettling events we had ever witnessed occurred. It was not something complex or obvious, like a floating ghost staring into the camera. No indeed. This was simple, yet the very nature of its simplicity was powerful and incredibly chilling. I showed the video clip to my skeptic-till-death husband. He stared in silence then said, "Incredible." We replayed it again and again.

Let's begin with the EVPs. One of the first happened just before the investigation began. The HGH team was on the third floor getting the equipment setup. Our audio captured a voice that, to us, had a slight German accent. It said, "Ja (yes), we can see this." It was almost as if more than one spirit watched. Could the spirit be confirming to the others that they could see what we were doing? We discovered on census records that the Whitneys employed German servants.

The next audio clip came just before the cleansing prayer. I went to get Bev on the second floor to ask her to join us on the floor above. Just after that we heard a voice, "Get out." Perhaps they didn't like us invading their space.

One additional EVP was recorded in the carriage house. This happened shortly after Maria felt an unsettled presence. Seconds after that, a roach was seen skittering across the floor. None of us could decipher

An EVP was captured in the carriage house

what the voice is saying, though it is clearly some kind of voice. You can listen to all of the EVPs in our Web site Secret Room.

Now for the video evidence. We mentioned that the second floor was the heart of activity. As it turns out, the stationary video camera on that floor was our link to the paranormal. It is rare to get video evidence. All too often the only thing you get from watching hours of video is a headache along with bugs and dust orbs.

The first piece of evidence was recorded near the end of the evening. Lisa's group was coming back from a break. You can hear their low voices on the first floor. It is during this moment, when the team is still downstairs, that footsteps are heard on the second floor. The lights on the second floor grand staircase turn off. Within the blink of an eye they were back on again. Moments later, Lisa's team is captured coming upstairs. There was no one on the second floor when the event happened. The cause remains unknown.

Last was the video clip that made my skeptic-till-death husband actually take note. It was recorded at the end of the investigation when Bev was alone on the second floor. She asked the spirits to give a response. Believing they had not, she headed downstairs, pausing briefly on the stairway to take one last photograph. At that very moment, almost on cue and unknown to her, Bev got a response. No one heard. From the second floor piano one lonely note, soft and deep, resonated into the darkness.

I recalled the story of Grace Whitney who had returned home too late to say goodbye to her father. She sat down at the piano and played. Her words rang in my mind, "If my father cannot see me, he will most certainly hear me play and know that I am here." Was it possible this simple piano note was a sign from Grace, or another member of the Whitney family? Was someone from the other side trying to tell us, *we're still here*?

A few months later, we all returned to the Whitney in an attempt to debunk the lights turning off and the sound of the piano. We also wanted to see if there was more evidence we could collect. We had a lot of activity on our first trip, and we were hoping the second would be as eventful.

Once again, the HGH team set up all of their equipment and took base EMF and temperature readings. Audio and video cameras were positioned in the same basic locations. Before teams began the actual investigation, Jenny and Lisa would attempt to identify natural causes for the evidence previously recorded.

First, Jenny and Lisa attempted to recreate the light turning off by the stairs. What they found is that it would have been very difficult for anyone to creep up the stairs without being seen by the lens of the stationary camera. However, it was possible if you stayed low and tightly hugged the wall.

Next, they tested the light source. The only light on that evening was the floor's security light, which had no on/off switch. A variety of tests were used to try and block the light. Nothing created the same effect as on the video.

Now they would move on to the piano note. There are several pianos at the Whitney. Two are on the third floor, one on the second, and one on the first floor. It seemed unlikely it came from the third floor. Lisa's group had been tearing down equipment and no one heard a note. We tested those pianos anyway. Only the concert piano could be heard, and no one from Lisa's group had been near it.

The piano on the first floor has a cover that creaks loudly when opened or closed. That sound was not recorded on the audio during the previous investigation.

The second floor piano, the floor that Bev was on, made a very good match. It was surprising and fascinating when notes were again heard from this piano during the second visit.

After being unable to disprove evidence from our first investigation, we got down to the second investigation. The evening would prove to be full of surprises.

At approximately 12:15 A.M. Keith, Dana, and Bev decided to go for a ride on the elevator. They hoped to sense, see, or hear something unusual. The threesome crowded in and pushed the button that would take them from the first to third floor. As the doors slowly closed, a feeling of apprehension grew. The quiet hum of the motors were heard as they began their ascent. It seemed to take forever. Finally, all a little relieved, the doors opened.

What the group did not know was the audio recorder on the elevator identified something else was with them. Recorded evidence would reveal a horrific scream. It seems nearly impossible that no one heard it.

A couple of hours later, Lisa and I moved into the Whitney's second floor dining room. Jenny stayed outside next to the piano.

Lisa and I walked to the back of the room and opened a small door. We found ourselves face-to-face with Mr. Whitney. It was his portrait, clipped on a pegboard in a small, unused kitchen. We stood, staring into his eyes as Jenny called out, "The piano. I just heard the piano!"

We quickly exited the small room as we heard Jenny asking, "If there's anyone that's over here, is there anyway you can do that again? I know that I just heard it, so I know you can do it again."

The three of us stood silent, waiting. How ironic the way it happened. Piano notes sounded just as we discovered the portrait of Mr. Whitney hidden away in the small kitchen. I remembered being shocked at seeing him there. I zoomed in on his face with my video camera. His eyes looked so alive... then Jenny's voice.

I focused my camera on the keyboard and checked the time. It was 2:52 A.M. EMF readings fluctuated slightly. I placed my audio recorder back on the piano, where it had been the entire evening up until at 2:30 A.M. when I turned it off.

Photograph Courtesy of The Whitney Restaurant

Mr. Whitney stares out   A piano note is heard at 2:52 A.M.

It was exciting yet unsettling. Our minds were racing, each with our own private thoughts. We remained on the floor for some time. No further notes were heard. As evidence would reveal, an audio recorder sitting across the room had captured the faint sounds. You can hear them in our Secret Room.

It seems about this same time, events were happening on the first floor. Bev was sitting by herself in a back, unlit dining room. She was quietly asking the Whitney family questions then asked for a sign of the presence with a knock. Bev patiently waited as seconds passed. Bang! The knock was loud and startling. She looked around. It sounded like it was right next to her. Thinking there was a simple explanation, she walked into the main hall. No one was on the first floor. Bev was alone. She felt a growing anticipating heading back to the room.

She calmly asked, "If that was you, can you do it again?"

Bang! The same knock sounded again. As she would find out the next day, shortly after the second knock a soft voice whispered, "Hello."

Perhaps one of the most revealing and startling pieces of audio material was sent to us by Jenny and Lisa just as Bev and I were finalizing this story. The audio was captured in the early morning hours on the second floor. Jenny, Lisa, and I were talking when, quite suddenly, I had felt a strange sensation. It is very difficult to explain the feeling other than an uncanny sense of something near. The atmosphere seemed to grow a bit heavier.

"Now, I'm getting something here. I'm getting something." I said.

In truth I had forgotten the incident since nothing remarkable seemed to happen at the time. Jenny and Lisa, however, discovered that my senses may have been correct. Just after I say, "I'm getting something,..." the first time, a voice whispers, "That's right." After I make the second statement, another distant voice, a different one, says, "I am still here."

Behind the laughter of the guests at this fine restaurant there is an unseen presence trying to reach out. It seems likely that there are more. It is said that granite creates a powerful energy with the ability to draw spirits. Could it be the massive granite walls of this estate that holds them here? Perhaps they simply don't want to leave, they just want us to know… *we're still here.*

Without a doubt, of all the investigations we've been on, The Whitney Restaurant is the most haunted location. What occurred to us is unexplainable and stunning. The volume of evidence collected is overwhelming. Highland Ghost Hunters has spent weeks of intense review of the audio and video collected and will continue their investigation of The Whitney. All photographic, audio, and video evidence will be posted in our Web site's Secret Room.

Grace Whitney Hoff

She has…the mystic's faith
that the unseen is more real than the seen.

As spoken by Dr. Samuel N. Watson, Paris, France

Excerpt from:
Grace Whitney Hoff:
The Story of An Abundant Life
By Carolyn Patch
1933

Story Two
Historic Fort Wayne

Barracks at Historic Fort Wayne

Detroit, Michigan
Web site: www.HauntedTravelsMI.com
Secret Room Password: fw728
Paranormal Investigative Team:
Metro Paranormal Investigations

Surrounded by the dense urban setting of a large city, hidden to most, is one of Detroit's most interesting landmarks, Historic Fort Wayne. In an effort to maintain the historical value of its past, the Historic Fort Wayne Coalition, a dedicated group of volunteers, is aggressively working to restore the decaying grounds and buildings. It is, to say the least, a daunting effort, but this committed group of people continues undeterred in their efforts.

Fort Wayne was considered a powerful, state-of-the-art military base after its construction in the 1840s. Though no battles were fought here, there are more than fifteen hundred recorded deaths along with many other unrecorded tragedies that may remain forever hidden within its crumbling walls.

Fort Wayne, circa 1861

Reprinted from Harpers Weekly, June 15, 1861

Chris and Wayne, from Metro Paranormal Investigations (MPI), asked us to join them for this investigation. They told us about reported incidents of paranormal activity since the 1890s. That definitely caught our attention. Add to that the opportunity of investigating such a historic place and we were ready to go.

What most people don't know is that the importance of this land pre-dates the building of the fort. It once was home to large Native American Indian populations. For hundreds of years before the White Man came, Chippewa, Huron, Ottawa, and Pottawatomie called this beautiful land along the river their home.

On or near the site that is now Fort Wayne were three of Michigan's largest Indian Burial Mounds. Native Americans deemed these sacred grounds of their ancestors, and to desecrate them was unthinkable. Yet, that is exactly what the white soldiers did… thoughtlessly and without care. During the fort's construction, two mounds were torn

Indian burial mound

up and the bones simply thrown away. Today, only one mound remains. It is the last remaining mound in the City of Detroit and is said to date back to 750 A.D.

Fort Wayne was initially built to protect Detroit from possible British attacks from Canada caused by a border dispute. As it turned out, the dispute did not result in military action and the fort remained vacant for several years. Ulysses S. Grant is said to have served as a lieutenant at the fort from 1849 to 1851.

It wasn't until the Civil War that the fort took on a significant role as an active military base. Since that time, the fort continued to serve as a military post until the early 1970s.

Of course, the Civil War is perhaps the fort's most active period. In 1861 it was set up as one of Michigan's key training and mustering posts. At the onset of the war, patriotism was at an all-time high. The atmosphere at the fort was almost jubilant with cheering crowds and marching bands. As the war progressed and the mass of wounded and dead began to arrive in Michigan, the mood changed.

Hospital battlegrounds like Chickamauga, Antietam, and Gettysburg were overwhelmed with wounded and dying soldiers. After a quick patch-up, those who were not dead were sent back to military hospitals away from the battlefields. Many never survived the trip back while others died shortly thereafter or languished for months or even years before succumbing to their wounds.

Military hospital now in ruins

The Fort Wayne hospital rooms were quickly filled and hallways lined with the wounded and dying. Finding a place to hold the growing number of bodies became a serious problem, and a "Dead House" was setup behind the hospital. As the war progressed, the fort's hospital was no longer able to handle the massive casualties, and Harper Hospital in Detroit took the overflow. Realities of the Civil War made it a dark time in Detroit.

After the war, things settled down and military life at the fort fell into a quiet routine. The quiet was soon broken, however, by one of the fort's most controversial incidents: the murder trial of Sergeant Clark.

It began with a young private by the name of Arthur Stone. Stone was considered intelligent, influential, and a leader in his company. He had been court-martialed, charged with seven counts of misconduct. The most serious charge was the private's false accusations against his sergeant and his continued perjury when he refused to recant his accusations.

Stone was sentenced to be dishonorably discharged and serve two years in prison for his actions. The young private continued to proclaim his innocence, swearing the accusations against his sergeant were accurate. After the court martial, Stone was held at Fort Wayne's guardhouse pending transfer to the prison on Governor's Island.

At approximately 7:00 P.M., July 12, 1887, guards were being relieved when Private Stone made a break for freedom. First Sergeant Clark was in charge that evening and ordered the private to halt. When he did not, Clark took a musket from a soldier and fired one ball over Stone's head. Clark then fired a second ball, aiming for Stone's leg, but his aim missed and the musket ball slammed into Stone's back. The power of the ball was so strong it blew a hole in Stone big enough to see through. The ball's path continued through the private's chest to plow up the ground twenty feet in front of him. He lived for several minutes, refusing to say anything except to give the name and location of his mother.

As it was later revealed, First Sergeant Clark was, in fact, the very sergeant the private had accused of unjust acts. The shooting was deemed suspicious. The United States court granted an order for the arrest of Sergeant Clark on one count of murder. Controversy grew when Fort Wayne's Colonel Black insisted the trial be held within the military courts. He refused to give up records and turn Clark over to the civil authorities. Eventually, Black was forced to release the case to the United States courts.

The trial was conducted. The presiding judge eventually determined that "…it was a justifiable act under the articles of war, as it was undisputed that Clark had no malice towards Stone and did not even know who he was. He could not know of what

Stone was shot in front of guardhouse/prison

crime the man attempting to escape was guilty, whether murder or larceny." Clark was found not guilty. It was a landmark case and a controversial decision.

For many, however, that was not the end. The controversy over the verdict and true intent of Clark remained in question by many in the community and in Private Stone's company. Though the judge determined Clark had not known the name of the soldier attempting escape, there were those who secretly believed Clark knew exactly who it was he shot. Clark's aim that evening was not off but true. It had been pure and simple murder.

We will never know if Clark got away with murder. Only his soul and that of Private Stone know the truth. Perhaps the spirits and the secrets they keep remain locked in the rooms of Fort Wayne's guardhouse.

Throughout the 1880s and 1890s, there were other reported accounts of violence and shootings. There is one account of an attempted escape of a Fort Wayne officer who was deemed legally insane. He was shot dead by a guard as he ran from the fort's hospital.

Smugglers, during late night and early morning hours, had become a problem during the early 1900s. They would bring black market oil, Opium, and liquor across the river from Canada. They would transport their illegal goods along the banks of the river on fort property. Skirmishes broke out, shots were fired, and soldiers were wounded.

Things changed again as the turn of the century passed and another war was declared. It was called, "The War to End All Wars," and, "The Great War." It was World War I and was the first war to take our soldiers overseas. The horrors of the war rapidly took a toll on our military. Then something even more monstrous eclipsed the injuries and death of the battlefield.

Soldiers began dying in large numbers from some unknown disease. Doctors were baffled. The disease struck suddenly with high fever, delirium, and nose bleeds. As the illness progressed, victim's faces turned blue, and they began to spit up blood. Doctors called it bloody pneumonia but knew it wasn't pneumonia.

It came to be known as the Spanish Influenza. Nearly eighty percent of U.S. military deaths during the war were from influenza. It seems strange today that something as simple as the flu would be considered a plague, but it was. In fact, it turned into a major worldwide pandemic.

Returning soldiers spread the virus across the United States. Michigan became a center for the illness. The halls of Fort Wayne's hospital were again filled with the sick and dying. Funeral processions leaving the fort were a daily occurrence.

At the height of the epidemic, the Red Cross began making daily rounds picking up the dead from porches where family members had placed them. Large areas were quarantined, and soldiers were required to wear masks when leaving the barracks.

Our state's governor cancelled all public gatherings. Within four months, tens of thousands within the city had been stricken and nearly four thousand died, many of those in Fort Wayne's hospital. Across the United States, nearly ten times more people died from the flu than in the war. We can only hope the United States and world will never be faced with another pandemic of this nature again.

Years passed and America enjoyed a carefree time called the "Roaring '20s." Indeed, the 1920s were a time of peace and prosperity. People forgot the horrors of war. Then came the Great Depression.

Just as it had after the Spanish American War, Fort Wayne became a refuge for many homeless women and children. Grave concerns arose over the fort's unsafe and unsanitary conditions. It wasn't until 1937 that the fort was actually given the funding to reclaim land along the river and improve living conditions in the buildings. Fort Wayne also served as a refuge for the homeless in 1940 and 1967 to 1971, after the Detroit riots.

Once military operations closed down in the 1970s, it became a military museum and served as a major Civil War re-enactment center through the 1980s. The fort went through some tough times in the late 1980s through early 1990s until the Detroit Historical Society began management. Currently, that responsibility falls into the able and committed hands of the Historic Fort Wayne Coalition.

Adding to the mystery of Historic Fort Wayne is something called the *Death Tunnels*. Few historians know of these tunnels. They are not part of the original blueprints. In fact, key members of the coalition swore they did not exist… until just recently. These tunnels are believed to run under what is now the fort's parking lot and exit somewhere in the city. Today, it is unknown where the entrances to these tunnels are or if they even still exist.

The Death Tunnels may have originally been designed for fast escape or to transport vital military supplies during attack. We have read Civil War accounts that speak of the tunnels as prisons used to hold traitors and military criminals.

Based on historical newspapers, hundreds if not thousands of rebel prisoners were imprisoned at the fort. There is also speculation they may have served the same purpose in World War I. It seems that the fort's sally ports or Death Tunnels were the most likely places to hold this number of prisoners.

These tunnels were said to be dark, damp, stagnant places without running water or hint of daylight. Many prisoners are believed to have died under these appalling, over crowed, unsanitary conditions with their bodies remaining undiscovered for days or weeks. It is hard to imagine the horror of such confinement.

Military reenactment

With initial research behind us, we were ready to join Chris and Wayne for our visit to this historic place. On this first visit, the guys were going to interview members of the coalition, get a tour of the facility, and gather more information about reported hauntings. Little did we know, when approaching its understated entrance, it would take us to a massive eighty-three-acre, star-shaped military complex and one of our most unforgettable experiences.

It was a beautiful mid-July day. Re-enactments of the Civil War were going on as we walked the grounds. It felt as though the very real spirits of those who had existed before surrounded us. Each re-enactor becomes a character from the Civil War. Even their conversations are typical of what you might expect from people of that era.

After we did our first walk-through, it became very clear that the investigation would pose a real challenge. MPI would need to determine how and where to set up equipment and position teams in this massive complex.

Wayne Miracle and Chris Forsythe making plans

Chris and Wayne met with Tom Berlucchi, Chairman of the Historic Fort Wayne Coalition, and Dave Demopoulos, Grounds' Manager, to review the fort's design and identify the most active locations. Based on this information, they came up with a

Dave Demopoulos and Tom Berlucchi give an overview of fort layout

plan to cover the fort. It would take several days to complete and would begin in late July.

The evening of our first investigation was another one of those extremely hot, humid, and deadly calm nights. It was the kind of heat that wrapped around you like a heavy, wet blanket. As the dark settled in, we stood outside the crumbling barrack walls and began to survey the vacant, dead shells that were once buildings filled with life. It seemed so different from our first visit.

Looking at the decaying structure that was once the fort's medical hospital and knowing its history made us wonder what may remain within its walls. Our group was eager to get inside to investigate. Unfortunately, the old hospital was in such decay that is was not safe. No one was permitted to enter. The team was disappointed, but the reality of what we would be facing became very clear.

MPI called in a team of more than fifteen people. The setup began. It would take hours to run hundreds of yards of wire and cord across the campus.

The focal points of the investigation were the prison, barracks, sally ports, and Indian mounds. Reported phenomena in these areas included disembodied voices, footsteps, strange sounds, apparitions, and doors opening or slamming shut.

We were divided into groups and assigned locations. Each team had a walkie-talkie to use for general communication and emergencies. Because of the dangerous conditions in many of the

A massive effort of people and equipment
was needed to cover the fort grounds

Barracks looked ominous at night

buildings, Chris and Wayne gave very specific safety and emergency instructions. They also emphasized the fact that there must be at least two people together at all times. No one was to go off alone. And so it began.

We stood in front of our first investigation site, the old barracks. Built in 1849, the barracks would hold two companies of soldiers (approximately two hundred to four hundred men). Though Kat and I are not frightened easily, we had to admit a bit of trepidation entering this deteriorated place. It was one of the oldest buildings at the fort, and its massive, multi-story appearance made the feeling more than a little overwhelming.   Another reason for trepidation is that on the hottest day of the summer, there was absolutely no ventilation in the building. All windows were tightly sealed. We knew the heat and humidity from the day would create an intense, sauna-like

Stairway leading to barracks' upper floors

atmosphere inside. The last reason became apparent as Chris led us up the dark, narrow stairways to upper floors. So many had walked these stairs before us. With each upward step, we felt the growing heaviness of their presence.

Gloomy barrack rooms

The third and fourth floors were supposedly the most active. We could understand why. Chipping paint, crumbling walls, and dust covered the loose floorboards and windowsills. If there were ghosts anywhere at the fort, it seemed likely they would be here. Or at least they *should* be here.

Why is it that ghosts always appear in the darkest, scariest places? Maybe it's because the atmosphere is right and our minds want to see them. The reason we were told is that spirits prefer quiet areas, and they retreat to those places that are most quiet, which usually means the ugliest section of the home or building. Whatever the cause, we knew that we would have to stay focused throughout this investigation to avoid mind tricks.

After a quick third floor walk-through, we settled in a back room to begin our EVP session. Each of us asked questions hoping for a response. The words were lost in the blackness of the room.

Floorboards creaked as Kat and Chris moved into the next room. I hung back for just a few seconds as something drew my attention to the room's inner wall. I couldn't explain what it was, just some sense. I began taking a series of pictures when my flash stopped. Feeling a little creeped-out, I suddenly remembered MPI's number one rule… *never be alone.* It occurred to me what a great and important rule that was. I quickly caught up with Kat and Chris. Only later would we discover what my camera had captured.

Our next assignment took the three of us to the sally ports. These are underground tunnels built as heavily fortified gateways so soldiers could rush out, attack enemies, and quickly retreat back to the fort. The massive wooden doors groaned as they were opened. We looked at each other and smiled. That was scary! The faint light from the night sky could not penetrate the ominous black within.

One of three sally port entrances

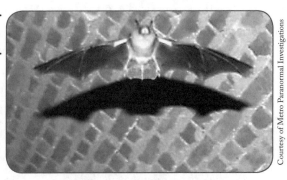

Sally port ghost... no a bat

As we entered the sally port, a rustling was heard in front of us. We were not alone. Our flashlights were little help. A black shape with piercing red eyes took form and darted through our weak circle of lights. We instinctively

The sally ports were a dark maze

Courtesy of Metro Paranormal Investigations

ducked and covered our heads as a bat swooped by and exited. We chuckled. Bats are a common occurrence in the sally ports.

We slowly moved through the chambers. At several points we stopped for EVP sessions. During those times, our flashlights were turned off and we remained in total darkness. Minutes passed in complete silence. It was like a tomb. The hour session seemed to last an eternity. Nothing happened, and we were happy for that.

Throughout the night, the teams continued going from one building to the next until the first rays of sunlight were seen. Everyone was exhausted and dehydrated from the heat. The atmosphere had been intimidating and overwhelming, but the spirits that evening seemed very elusive. This, Chris explained to us was a typical investigation. "It's mostly just sitting and listening. It can get pretty boring, but capturing that one piece of evidence makes it all worthwhile." Chris and Wayne planned the next investigation for the following weekend.

Not much had changed in seven days. It was another hot and steamy Friday evening. Saturday wasn't going to be any better. When we arrived, the MPI team had the equipment set up, and

The Spanish guardhouse

we were ready to go. The plan on this investigation was to cover not only the main fort but to expand the investigation to include some of the outer buildings.

One of our planned stops was the fort's Spanish-styled guardhouse. It was here that Private Stone had been shot dead by Sergeant Clark. In addition to the Stone killing, there were other reports of soldiers being shot and killed during desperate escapes from these prison cells.

The original building was constructed in 1889. It had reports of frequent activity. Some of the phenomena that supposedly occur include jail doors opening and closing. Disembodied voices have also been heard. The jail was relatively small compared to the other buildings. Inside were four narrow cells meant to hold the most dangerous prisoners. On the sides were community cells for less serious offenders. It was a little unsettling in the dark to watch and wait. Time passed, and our experience was uneventful.

It was some time after midnight when Wendy, from MPI, and I were sent to one of the three-story outer buildings. Its neglected exterior covered in overgrown bushes only gave us a hint of what to expect inside. Pulling away the shrubbery, we entered and were shocked at what we saw. The floors were literally covered with layers of broken glass, plaster, wood, and garbage. Old furniture was strewn everywhere. The air was filled with mold and dust, making it difficult to breath.

We carefully climbed the narrow, rotting staircase fearing it would collapse at any moment. There was no handrail, so we hugged the wall. Planning to work our way down, we passed the second floor entrance

Some buildings are in very bad condition

stopping, finally, at the third floor and came to an abrupt halt. The floor was missing.

Retreating to the second floor Wendy laughed, "I think we've found the third floor." She was right. The shattered remains of the upper floor lay in massive chunks everywhere. There was obviously no way we could stay, so we headed down.

The heat and oppressive conditions were overwhelming on the first floor. Wendy and I stopped briefly for a little EVP session. It was becoming too difficult to breathe, so we left. Once outside, we started to laugh, happy just to be alive. It's interesting that neither of us really thought about our EVP session until the audio was reviewed several weeks later.

On the last day of investigation, Jo and Kat began their assignment in the "Lemon House," just outside the fort walls. It is a multi-level building that the group had named for the lemonade stand that had stood in front of it during the re-enactment event a few weeks earlier. Its original purpose remains a mystery. What made this building unique was its complex spider web of rooms. There were very few hallways. One room led into another, which led into another, and so on. It was easy to get lost.

The Lemon House was a maze of doorways

The first floor had undergone major renovations and was surprisingly fresh and clean. Jo and Kat soon discovered it was in complete contrast to the other levels. A sense of foreboding began as they ascended the narrow stairway to the upper floors.

Untouched for many decades, dust clouded the air and clung to the remnants of remaining furniture. They snaked through the maze of rooms; it was hard to understand the purpose of so many small, closet-sized areas. Most were too small to fit even a single bed.

Jo's sense of unease began the moment they entered the second floor and grew as they moved upward. Jo does not consider herself to be a psychic but does feel she has some sensitivity. She couldn't explain what she was feeling or why, but the feeling was unsettling and heavy.

Earlier in the investigation Deana took readings in the Lemon House

The two continued their exploration, audio and video recorders running. There were no sounds or movements, nothing unusual, yet Jo's tension continued to grow. Finally, she turned to Kat and said, "You know, I have got to get out of here." One look at Jo's pale face told Kat everything, and she nodded in agreement. Only thirty minutes into the investigation, they left. Once outside, Jo whispered, "I don't know what it was about that place. It was just oppressive. I didn't like it." Kat hoped something interesting would turn up on audio or video.

In the early hours of the morning, teams reassembled for a break before the final assignments were given. People were exhausted. It was time to re-hydrate and eat some snacks.

Beef jerky, crackers, and Cheez Whiz flew like orbs in a dusty room. Next came the fresh fruit and veggies to make us feel healthy. It wasn't only eating junk food. There was also junk food discussion. We were told beef jerky was significant both nutritionally and in American culture. Kat and I did not know that.

Then came the question, do cherries have more vitamins than apples? Are seedless melons tastier than ones with seeds? Yes, we had spent too many hours sitting in the sweltering dark, surrounded by mold, talking to no one, and getting no answers. The groups sat in a circle laughing, passing the snacks around, and joking about how old we all felt. The break was over much too soon.

Wayne and Chris gave out the last assignments for the evening, and each group headed out. Deana and I set off to the Indian burial grounds, and Kat and Jo headed for the old barracks.

Faint light from the moon reflected across the mounds. Shadows from trees and shrubs shrouded the area with an ominous spirituality. We reflected on those who once owned this land.

No one is certain who built the mounds, not even Native Americans. Legend has it that it was the mark of an evil civilization called the Yam-Ko-Desh (Ottawa name for Prairie People) that was eventually defeated and driven off by the ancestors of today's native tribes. In honor of those who had defeated the evil Yam-Ko-Desh, the mounds were considered a sacred place for burial.

Even now some will warn you to stay away from these *sacred places*. To quote an elderly Native American, "It is not good that you go to the place of the Yam-Ko-Desh." He insists that disturbing his ancestors will release the evil spirits that once roamed there.

Deana and I spent nearly an hour at this sacred location where voices had been reported. A slight breeze picked up rustling the leaves in the trees. We listened intently in case this was an omen of things to come. We detected nothing.

Meanwhile, on the opposite side of the fort, Kat and Jo were exploring the old barracks. Since Kat had been there before, she led Jo through the various floors. After briefly reviewing the first and second levels, they moved to the third.

Resting on a window ledge, Jo scanned the darkened room and whispered, "I can feel them here… the soldiers. I can see them talking to each other after a busy day, just shooting the breeze. Nothing bad, in fact I feel a lot of positive energy here." Jo sat in silence for several moments.

Kat quietly moved into the next room where a light bulb hung from a single wire in the middle of the room. Aiming her video camera at it she asked, "If there is someone here with us, can you move the light? Go ahead, move it. Let us know you're here." Then, "Are you afraid? Don't be afraid." She held her camera on the light for some time. So focused on observing any movement in the light bulb, Kat missed what was an important single response. Fortunately, her video did not miss it.

It was sometime after 2:30 A.M. when Kat and Jo reached the fourth floor attic. By far, this was the worst area. Dark, cramped rooms were filled with the smell of decay. It was almost

A portion of the wall of names, old barracks

claustrophobic. They entered a room with a low, sharply slanted ceiling. Pealing paint and chunks of plaster hung from the walls and lay scattered on the floor.

Though Kat had been here before, her flashlight caught something on the walls and ceiling she had not previously noticed. Scratched into the plaster were names and dates. She and Jo realized it was the graffiti of soldiers. Some dated back to the 1800s.

Jo began reading the names. It was then Kat felt a cool breeze across the back of her neck. It was refreshing until she realized there were no open windows or even a hint of a breeze in the stifling atmosphere. Kat mentioned this to Jo who replied, "I just felt a cool breeze on my cheek." Several seconds later Jo's camera began to beep. "Oh, my battery just died," she said. It was then Kat thought she heard something. A whisper? Kat looked around but there was no one there.

Some time later the sound of Jo's walkie-talkie cracked, and they heard Chris calling in the teams. The investigation was a wrap.

We have mentioned several times that evidence review is tedious and time consuming, so we don't have to mention it again. Well, it seems we just did. Needless to say, it took us several weeks and MPI several months to thoroughly review hours and hours of audio, video, and photos.

Well over fifteen hundred photographs were taken over the three-day period. While most came back with little results, there were a couple of very interesting photographs.

MPI's photo was shocking, to say the least. It clearly showed an apparition in a sally port. The photo had been taken around 6:30 P.M. on a cloudless day.

Courtesy of Metro Paranormal Investigations

Possible apparition

Many groups would automatically call it a ghost. MPI is not that type of group. They went back the next day at exactly the same time with exactly the same people and recreated the scene down to the smallest detail. After careful analysis, the ghostly image is believed to be a member of their team. Further examination is being conducted. Very few groups are as thorough as MPI.

Another interesting photo is one taken from the third floor of the old barracks. This was the series of photos I had taken after Chris and Kat moved into another room. I am not sure why I hung back to takes those pictures, but I did.

The first few photos were completely black. The next three photos showed something very unusual. An orange glow appeared, changing to an orange swirl that strangely turned to blue in the third photograph. This anomaly expanded upward, and a surprising shape descended from it. The shape appears to be a face. Or is it? It could be simple camera movement creating an anomalous light swirl. Is the vision of a face an example of matrixing (matrixing is where the mind sees images in unfamiliar, random shapes)? We have the black and white photo here, but you can see the full color series of photographs in our Secret Room.

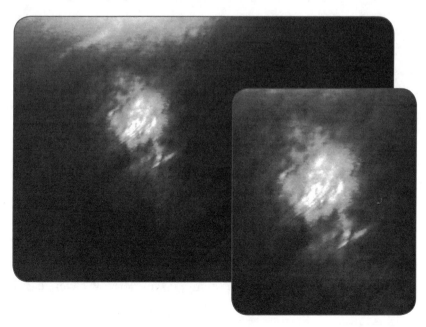

Room where the strange lights appeared

MPI carefully reviewed hours of video, but nothing significant was discovered. Kat was the only one to capture something on video. It was during the time that she and Jo were in the barracks. Kat had focused her video camera on a light bulb hanging from a slender wire.

In an attempt to encourage a response, Kat made the statement, "Are you afraid? Don't be afraid." It was after that something curious happened. A light appeared below the suspended bulb. It then vanished. It might have been a reflection from the camera's infrared light. However, Kat had the camera focused steadily on the bulb for some time, without a similar reoccurrence. No one else was in the room with them, and there were no windows. The video clip can be seen in our Secret Room.

Perhaps one of the more unsettling bits of evidence came from audio. Chris stopped by for the reveal. We sat quietly as he played the first audio clip. A team leaving the tunnel near an Indian burial mound collected the audio. The sound was very faint, the hushed whisper of a man's voice clearly saying, "Over here." We were eager to hear more.

The second audio took place in the Lemon House where Jo had been very uneasy. Kat and Jo were kidding abut collecting evidence when a raspy, unearthly voice cut in, "It's not gonna happen." It was particularly unnerving that the voice sounded almost inhuman and seemed to respond to their conversation. Perhaps it was this eerie presence that Jo had sensed in the house.

The third EVP was taken when Wendy and I were in an outer building. This was the building without a third floor. Though we were not there very long, an EVP was captured. The words were spoken in a gruff voice, typical of what you might expect from a weary soldier. Three simple words were heard that contained a graphic curse. The statement is not printed here because of its adult content but can be heard in our Web site's Secret Room.

The fourth audio was simple, recorded in the early morning hours in the barracks. No one was there at the time. It was a loud bang, like the sound of a door slamming. Did this represent a paranormal event or was it simply something falling down in an old building?

Kat had collected other bits of audio evidence at the barracks. The first was captured when Jo had sensed the feelings of past soldiers on the floor. The EVP was a male voice barely audible, but words could be understood after some adjustments. The first hushed voice said, "Take fire from the enemy." The other whispered, "It's a lie."

The last bit of evidence came as a very unsettling surprise to Kat. It was this next experience that began changing Kat's skeptical belief in ghosts and hauntings. It had been collected when she and Jo were in the attic. They were reading out loud the names of soldiers etched in the ceiling. Jo's camera had suddenly failed, and Kat had thought she'd heard a whisper. She was right. There, recorded on the video camera's audio, was a ragged breath. It was close, very close, to the camera and to Kat. Distinctively male, it obviously did not come from either of the women. Had the energy of a soldier tried to respond to his name? You can hear all the recorded audio evidence in our Web site's Secret Room.

There is no doubt our investigation of Historic Fort Wayne was fascinating and one of our more interesting trips. Who knows what actually happened within the crumbling walls of this once powerful place. What tragedies and events occurred that might never be known? Much of the records have been lost to time. What seems certain is that something unexplainable is going on at the fort. Is it the spirits of those who have passed or an unknown phenomena that has yet to be understood? MPI will continue their investigation and updates will be posted in our Secret Room.

MPI and us… so happy together

Story Three
The Locker Room Saloon

Utica, Michigan
Web site: www.HauntedTravelsMI.com
Secret Room Password: r628u
Paranormal Investigative Team:
Metro Paranormal Investigations

It was a hot, summer morning, the day after Beer and Pizza Night at the Locker Room Saloon in the historical little town of Utica, Michigan. Mornings come too early the day after Beer and Pizza Night.

We turned on our computers and leisurely sipped coffee and watched the approach of dark storm clouds. Of course, we had to get to work. The creative juices began to flow as my fingers swiftly typed the first sentence, "Bev slowly pulled the drumstick from her hair the morning after Beer and Pizza Night…"

"Well for crying out loud, that's ridiculous! No one will understand what that means!" Bev said, as she slowly pulled the drumstick from her hair.

Bev was right, of course. That's why we decided to begin this story on a lighter note by first telling you about the high-octane fun that happens every night at the Locker Room Saloon.

This is not just a normal neighborhood pub. It's a party bar. During early evenings, families will frequently stop for dinner. Later, however, the party kicks up a notch for adults of all ages. It's a great place to go if you need a good laugh and want to forget about the day's stress.

Always packed on Beer and Pizza Night

While every night is party night at the Locker Room, Wednesday is Beer and Pizza Night. $3.50 will buy you a personal thin or regular crust pizza and a bucket of ice with three longnecks of your choice. The pizza is their own special recipe and really excellent. The beers are cold.

Now, before we go much further, let's talk about the drumsticks. They aren't just a hair ornament, though they were for Bev on this lazy summer morning. Actually, most nights, the DJ notches-up the music, and drumsticks are given to everyone to pound out the rhythm on the tables, walls, or even your friend sitting next to you.

After the drumsticks come out, everyone at the Locker Room gets ready for the party. Waiters and bartenders are definitely a fun-loving group who really come alive with fast music and beating drumsticks. They'll mix your favorite drink standing on the bar, flipping bottles to one another while they dance to the music or creating their amazing waterfall drink mixes (you can check out their waterfall at our Web site's Secret Room). By the end of the night, the whole place is laughing and partying without any worries. No one would ever guess that this spot was the very location where one of Utica's most horrific disasters began... the fire of 1904.

Let us begin before that terrible day... back to 1834. Utica was a little dirt town that had gone through several name changes, including McDougalville, Hogs Hollow, and Harlow. On this very location that is now the Locker Room stood The Exchange Hotel.

Brothers Gurdon and Payne Leech, who were also responsible for giving this town its current name of Utica, built the hotel as a two-story stagecoach stop. Gurdon and Payne built the first Exchange Hotel for the town's sheriff, George E. Adair, and his family. It changed hands several times. By the mid-nineteenth century, the new owner, B.C. Gunn, expanded the hotel making it a four-story, luxury lodging with a large stable. Over its life, The Exchange hosted some of Michigan's most prominent citizens, business leaders, and politicians. It remained a focal point of the city until the great fire of 1904.

It was a beautiful spring morning on Sunday, May 8, 1904. A strong southerly breeze swept through the near-empty streets of the small town. Most of its 580 residents were observing the Sabbath.

A local town vagrant, Joe Weinburger, had spent the cool night in the Exchange Hotel's stable. Joe apparently took advantage of the stable on occasion, much to the chagrin of its landlord, Mr. W. Cole. Joe's smoking was particularly troublesome to Mr. Cole, who was always concerned about fire and the safety of the horses. Even the townsfolk worried about fire since most of the small community's buildings were wood framed.

On this particular morning, Mr. Cole was in no mood to see Joe. He showed his displeasure by dousing the vagrant with a couple of buckets of water. Joe skedaddled.

It was shortly after that, around 9:30 A.M., the fearful cry of fire was heard as smoke began to billow from the stable. Winds quickly drew the fire to the adjacent Exchange Hotel. Within minutes its wooden frame became a seething inferno. Rapidly, hot embers drifted to the wooden rooftops of nearby buildings. New fires were almost instantly ignited.

Courtesy of the Utica Sentinel, May 20, 1904

The Exchange Hotel, circa 1850

Townsfolk rushed to form bucket brigades. Water was taken from horse troughs, nearby creeks, and the millstream. Residents and business owners worked feverishly in dazed silence to control the blaze. One of the town's wealthiest men, William Upton, was knocked unconscious when he fell three stories in a valiant effort to extinguish the flames. William remained unconscious for over thirty hours after the incident.

It was a great relief to the weary townspeople when they saw the train arrive with the Detroit Fire Department's fire wagon to help with the effort. In fact, the town was so excited, the fire department had to turn hoses on the massing crowds to move them back before they could unload the wagon from the train.

When the last flames were extinguished and the smoke had cleared, the entire heart of Utica was gone. The Exchange Hotel had turned into a pile of cinders.

The town's rebuilding process began almost immediately. Unfortunately, one year later, also on a Sunday, another fire tore through Utica. The Exchange was never rebuilt, and the land lay vacant for more than a decade. In 1915 James V. Clinesmith purchased the land and built a new hotel on the site. That same building is currently the Locker Room Saloon, located on the corner of Cass and Auburn Road.

It was difficult to put together an accurate history of the property

The Exchange Hotel after the fire

Rebuilt hotel, circa 1915

between 1915 and the 1980s. After weeks of reviewing old newspaper archives and working with various historical groups, a definitive history could not be traced. There are, however, stories of what happened to the property once known as The Exchange Hotel.

It served as a World War I military hospital and, for a time, a girls' school. At some point it became an office building and, since the mid-1980s, has been owned by the Pittman family who currently operate the Locker Room Saloon.

We first heard about the saloon's paranormal activity from Chris and Wayne, co-founders of Metro Paranormal Investigations (MPI). According to recent claims, a ghostly old woman is seen staring out of a second-story window facing Shelby Road. There are also frequent reports of unknown voices, footsteps, doors closing, and lights turning on unexpectedly. When MPI asked us to join them on their next investigation, we eagerly accepted.

We arrived at the Locker Room just before sunset on Sunday. It had been an incredibly hot and humid day with temperatures rising past the mid-90s. There was little relief as evening approached.

Sweat broke out on our brows the minute we left our air-conditioned cars. There would be no relief tonight in the Locker Room's normally cool interior. Air-conditioning and other electrical systems and/or motors were turned off. This was done to keep noise-levels down for audio recordings during EVP (electronic voice phenomena) collection and to reduce EMF (electro-magnetic field) spikes caused by electrical currents.

The bar, usually alive with laughter and loud music was eerily hushed tonight. Soft voices were heard from members of the MPI team as they assembled their equipment.

Chris and Wayne met us at the door and introduced us to the key members of the team for this investigation, which included Wendy, Deana, Erin, Chris, Kevin, and Kristy. Before our arrival, the group had already set up video cameras and wireless audio in the designated active areas.

On this night, Chris and Wayne had invited a special guest to join their group. Rita is a psychic that MPI occasionally uses

Wayne Miracle and Chris Forsythe give last minute instructions

on investigations. She had not been given any information on the location or its history before her arrival. Tonight, Rita would use her enhanced senses to pick up energies, feelings, or possible identities of the spirits that might remain.

Chris and Wayne assembled the group to briefly go over the night's game plan. Rita would do an initial walk-through. At the same time, teams of two or three would be assigned to various locations in the basement and first and second floors to initiate private investigations.

We joined Wendy as she and Rita began their tour of the basement. The heat and humidity followed us as our group descended the stairs into blackness. The basement showed its age and history with every step. Decades of time slipped away.

Rita immediately picked up on something and moved to the first small room to her right. She sensed fear and people being confined. She rapidly moved to other sections of the basement, each time repeating the words, "Fire... I see more than one fire." In another section, Rita sensed the presence of a man who, she felt, had seriously injured his head and "...wasn't quite right after that." She also sensed a woman. Someone who looked prim and proper but, "Honey, when she stepped out, she was really something else."

Returning to the main floor, Rita entered the kitchen. Here she picked up the energy of a man. She sensed he was a friendly, jovial sort… dark hair, liked to wear suspenders and talk about women in a rather crude way. After some time, she moved to the top floor. In one of the side rooms Rita felt the presence of an older woman gazing out the window. This older woman, "… liked to watch the carriages pass by," she said.

Rita Sacco senses fear and confinement

Rita senses the 1904 fire

After the walk-through, David (Oz) Pittman, one of the bar's owners, sat down with Rita to talk about her experiences. Surprisingly, much of what she had said held merit. In the basement's small room, where Rita had sensed fear and confinement, Dave confirmed that people had been held

Dave (Oz) Pittman, an owner, talks about the haunting

there during a robbery several years back. The man in the kitchen with suspenders and the crude talk about women fit the description of a long-time cook at the bar that had since passed away. The man injuring his head could well have been Mr. Upton, who fell three stories during the fire of 1904 and remained unconscious for thirty hours. The prim and proper woman who was a bit of tart and the older woman upstairs is still a mystery. They could easily have been associated with the girls' school or a former guest from the hotel's earlier days when long-term residents were not uncommon. A video of Rita's encounters with the spirits can be found on our Web site's Secret Room.

It would be some time after Rita left that the investigation became more intense. Bev was stationed in the basement with Dave, Chris, and Wayne. The oppressive heat made the darkness claustrophobic and almost unbearable. Intense silence was broken with questions given to possible unknown spirits around them. There was no response. Time slipped away as did patience. Their final question into the emptiness asked for one simple response before they left. Again, silence. As the group stood to leave, a light appeared behind them.

Chris, Oz, and Wayne discuss the activity

They all turned in surprise. "Who turned on the computer?" Dave whispered.

In fact, there before them, the computer screen glowed like a signal beacon in the darkness. Was it a response to their last question or just an electrical surge? Dave went to his computer and shut it down. He attempted to restart it by moving cords, wires, keyboard, and mouse. He shuffled his feet against the

The computer mysteriously turned on

rug attempting to create static electricity that might trigger the computer to re-start. Nothing seemed to have an effect. Amazingly, later that evening, the computer did turn on again. At that time, one of the team members reported feeling something cold brush past his leg and noted the room growing suddenly cooler.

The investigations continued through the night. It was in the early morning hours that something quite interesting happened to Chris and Wayne. They were stationed on the third floor. The air was particularly heavy and motionless here and seemed even more oppressive than on the other floors.

Both men sat quietly, their eyes peering into the gloom, their ears listening for the slightest sound. Something caught Chris' attention: a movement, slight though clearly visible. He signaled to Wayne, pointing forward. Wayne instantly picked up on it. Before their eyes, the stationary camera's cable, suspended above the floor, began to sway. It lasted briefly, a few seconds at best, then stilled once more. There was no apparent cause for this movement. Regretfully, the event had not been recorded on video. According to MPI standards, it had to be placed in the "personal experience" category, which means it cannot be used to verify paranormal activity.

MPI reveals the evidence to Dave

During the investigation, there were numerous personal experiences. These included footsteps on stairways, the sound of bottles moving, and the smell of unusual fragrances. There had also been several sudden battery failures, though no unusual EMF or temperature fluctuations had been recorded.

All in all, it had been an interesting evening. The big question remained, had there been any documented evidence collected?

The tedious process of evidence review began in the following days. The first run-through of audio, video, and still materials didn't reveal anything significant. Now, here's where real-life paranormal investigators differ from the ones you see on TV. The first go-through is never the last. Recorded material is usually reviewed several times before a determination is made.

It wasn't until the third review that the first documented audio evidence was identified. It had been recorded on the second floor. We looked at each other in surprise. The first EVP appeared to be two people, a male and female. The male rasped, "Here they are." The female seemed to respond, "Who are?" The voices matched none of the members of the team. MPI had captured solid evidence.

A male voice is heard in another clip. Wayne is talking about a recent investigation the MPI team had completed. He said that it had been cold, below zero, during the investigation. It is then the raspy whisper of a male voice is heard. At first, it sounded like, "It's alive." A chill ran through us. We listened to the audio again. Replaying it several times, it began to sound more like, "That's a lie." Was the voice responding to Wayne's comment?

Of course, we have saved the most interesting documented evidence for last. It occurred in the basement at 12:35 A.M. This was the exact time when everyone was outside taking a break. The building was completely empty. A stationary video camera was positioned near the basement's back wall. It covered the main storage area. In the center of the video was a light bulb with pull string. This was an area were MPI had captured unusual light anomalies during a previous investigation.

Initially, nothing seemed out of order. Then, we saw something on video. The movement was simple and brief. The light cord suspended from the ceiling... plucked from the middle like a guitar string. Then the camera, securely fixed to the table, jumped. It was as if some unseen, yet powerful, energy passed over it. This video clip can be seen in our Secret Room.

The investigation of the Locker Room Saloon continues even as we finish writing this story. There is much more to be discovered in this seemingly unlikely place for ghosts to reside.

Are these spirits that remain or some unknown, natural force that we simply don't understand? Certainly we did not see a moving apparition or ghostly faces. Does that mean that something paranormal doesn't exist at the Locker Room Saloon?

We pondered this as we sit here on this hot summer day with a storm raging outside. We listen to the powerful winds slam against our window and watch as the trees bent like slender reeds. We can't see the wind... does that mean it doesn't exist?

The light string moved... Was it paranormal?

Story Four
Sweet Dreams Inn
Victorian Bed & Breakfast

Bay Port, Michigan
Web site: www.HauntedTravelsMI.com
Secret Room Password: w6bq6
Paranormal Team:
Metro Paranormal Investigations

Little did we know this investigation would take us in an unexpected direction. Events that transpired are mystifying and more intriguing than the best fiction story. Except this was not fiction but very real and very true. Let's begin at the beginning.

Kat and I were reviewing information people had sent of places with reported paranormal activity. Looking through our stack of photographs, we came across one that immediately caught my attention. It was a Victorian-style bed and breakfast near Lake Huron in a little town called Bay Port.

It's hard to explain my initial feelings about the inn except that I felt drawn to it. I mentioned to Kat it looked vaguely familiar and asked if it was one of the lodgings in our other book, *Michigan Vacation Guide*. This is a book we've written since 1991. It features unique places to stay while vacationing in Michigan. Along with private cottages, homes, and resorts, it also includes a number of bed and breakfasts. Since it looked familiar, I wondered if this bed and breakfast was one of them.

Kat looked at the photo and shook her head. "No, I don't think so, but let me check." She quickly scanned our property owner database and found it was not one of our lodgings. She also mentioned that, according to records, we've never been to Bay Port. Chuckling, we joked about how, after a while, it's easy to lose track of where you've been and what you've seen.

Kat contacted the innkeeper, Julie, to gather some information on reported paranormal activity. Julie confirmed that both her family and guests have experienced frequent and considerable activity at the home.

The most common phenomena are the sounds of children laughing and crying, footsteps, and doors opening and closing. Sounds of music have also been heard from the third floor. Other unusual activities include drawers slamming and loud bangs. She then recounted an unsettling experience her daughter had in the outdoor log-cabin playhouse a few years back.

Made from actual logs, the playhouse is tall enough for adults to stand inside and even has a cute, wood-burning fireplace. Julie's daughter and a friend thought it would be fun to have a sleepover

Log cabin playhouse

in this cozy little log cabin. The girls didn't stay the night. After several hours they returned to the home frightened, saying they could hear a woman screaming, "…like she was being murdered." That was the first and only time her children would go near the playhouse.

Julie believes the most active area of the home is room number two. It's now called the Peacock Room, but Julie frequently refers to it by the original name, the Rose Room. Here objects have been seen moving or flying off shelves. A few of her guests and friends reported waking to the feeling of being pushed out of bed. According to Julie, nearly half of her guests leave in the middle of the night. Julie said, "I'll wake up in the morning, and they'll just be gone."

When Kat asked her about the history of the home, Julie didn't have a lot of information. She only knew it had been built around the turn of the century by a wealthy man named William Wallace. She knew Mr. Wallace had a wife and children but not much more than that. Julie attempted to collect historical data at the library with little success.

Before conducting the initial investigation, we did some additional research and learned that William Wallace was indeed

a prominent businessman who
owned and managed one of the
area's largest, most successful
stone quarries. He actually had
his hands in quite a few other
business ventures including
the Bay Port Fish Company
and Bay Port Bank.

We noted he was married
twice and had seven children,
Nellie, Belle, Robert, William,
Frances, Ora, and Margaret.
His second wife's name was
Margaret.

We were perplexed that we
could find nothing in census
data or death records regarding
William's first wife. She was a
mystery. We did come across
an old 1893 newspaper article that mentioned, "Mrs. W. Wallace
had died suddenly at the age of 27." We grew even more frustrated
when we couldn't find exact cause of death or even her first name.

Courtesy of Liz Montgomery, Wallace family descendant

William H. Wallace

We did know her last child, Billy, was born the year she died. At
this time, however, we weren't able to find the month of his birth.
We vaguely wondered if the first Mrs. Wallace had died during
childbirth. This was not uncommon in those days.

Certainly more research would be required later but, for now, the
place sounded very interesting and an investigation was scheduled
for early fall. We contacted Metro Paranormal Investigations
(MPI) for this project. Chris and Wayne, as always, were more
than happy to help.

Our journey began on a crisp autumn day. The drive took us
past farms and quiet wooded landscapes. My original feeling about
having previously been to Bay Port immediately vanished when
we got lost. Really, we had no idea where we were. There wasn't
even a McDonalds or gas station to ask directions.

We came to a road temporarily closed to construction. A barrier blocked us from entering and threatened legal prosecution. Barrier be damned, we broke the law and drove around it. A few minutes later, as if the hand of fate smacked us across the face, we found Sweet Dreams. Actually, it isn't hard to find for the vast majority of people, just those of us directionally challenged.

As we pulled into the driveway, Julie was waiting at the door. She waved and came to greet us saying that the MPI team had already arrived and left for dinner.

Following her inside, she turned and jokingly apologized for the newly painted pink exterior. "Really" she said, "it didn't look this pink when I selected it." We laughed. It really wasn't *that* pink; besides, freshly painted homes always look nice.

Julie gave us a tour of the grounds while we waited for the MPI crew to return. The home's interior had a simple, comfortable feel. I felt right at home. As Kat and Julie continued to chat, I went directly to the second door on the right and headed upstairs. Turning left at the top of the stairs, I immediately moved towards the Peacock Room and entered. A brief sense of déjà vu passed over me. The view from the windows showed the lake beyond and brought happy memories of warm summer days at the beach.

Welcoming room is said to be paranormally active

Soon after, Julie and Kat joined me. Kat passed by and smiled, "Well, you certainly made yourself at home here. Could have waited for us." I laughed and began photographing the rooms while Julie continued to give Kat a tour and brief history.

The third floor was divided into a large living room and two bedrooms. Surprised, I thought it would be a wide-open area. It was a nice, private place for a family to stay and, at the time of our visit, only $150 a night.

I finished photographing the floor and followed Julie and Kat outside to the log cabin playhouse. Even in some disrepair, the interior of the cabin was still a remarkably cute little place with miniature table and chairs set up for a little tea party. A full-size sofa sat against one wall and a small fireplace against the other. I quickly took a couple of photos and left.

It was just about then that the MPI caravan of cars pulls in the driveway. We greeted each other like old friends. It was great to be working with them again.

Julie had already given Chris, Wayne, and the crew a tour of the home, pointing out areas of reported phenomena. Based on the information Julie provided, Chris and Wayne laid out instructions for the evening's investigation, which included placement of equipment and assignments. Teams would stay on each floor of the home and the playhouse, and they would rotate every hour. MPI rapidly completed setups and checks. Within a short time it went dark.

Wendy, from MPI, and I would be partners for the evening and headed up to the third floor. Neither of us sensed anything unusual upon our arrival. We explored the rooms before settling in the main living area.

The innkeeper and Chris Forsythe kid around

It was around 8:30 P.M. when we began to call out the names of the Wallace children. I ended by talking to Ora. We sat intently listening for any audible response. Initially, all was silent until, directly behind us, there was a loud boom that sounded very much like a heavy book slamming to the floor.

Wendy and I jumped in surprise, immediately searching each room to see if anything was out of place. Nothing was found. Standing vigilant for several moments, our eyes scanned the darkness. No further sounds were heard.

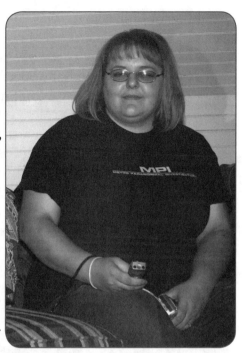

Wendy's recorder didn't capture the bang heard on the third floor

What we didn't know was that at the same time we heard the bang, Deana and Kat were experiencing a phenomena of their own on the main floor. Deana was positioned on the sofa across the room from Kat, who sat in a chair by the window.

Conducting EVPs, Kat asked William's first wife if she missed not knowing her youngest child, Billy. At the time of our investigation,

Deana felt an unusual heaviness in the living room

we didn't know if she died during childbirth or after Billy was born. In either case, she wouldn't have been around to see him grow up. It was then Deana experienced a warm, overwhelming sensation press down on her. When Kat stopped talking, the warm pressure went away. Deana asked Kat to continue, but the pressure did not return.

Everyone regrouped after the first session. Though details were not shared, it appeared the evening was relatively quiet for the rest of the group. After a delicious, nutritious snack and some water, Chris and Wayne assigned teams to the next location.

Our assignment began around 10:00 P.M. on the second floor. This time Karen, another MPI member, joined Wendy and me. I suggested we start in room number four, the Sarah Rose Room.

This was a charming little spot with an open lace canopy bed. Three small chairs, a dresser and tables lined the walls. Washed in soft moonlight, it was possible for us to see each other and our surroundings.

The Sarah Rose Room

Time to get down to work. Wendy and Karen took turns talking to the children, speaking their names, and asking questions. All remained quiet, no response.

After some time, I decided to give it a try. I called out the name of the first child. The three of us were instantly alert.

"Did you see what I just saw?" I said.

Wendy and Karen nodded yes. Ever so softly, the lace at the foot of the bed moved. The movement was only slight but clearly visible to all of us. Was it mere coincidence? I called out another name and waited. The lace moved again.

Wendy immediately checked the room's heating and air vents as well as windows to see if airflow or drafts were causing the movement. They were not. We waited several minutes in silence watching the lace. It did not move.

During the next half-hour, I called to the children on several more occasions, and each time the lace gently swayed. No one reported cold spots or unusual feelings. We hoped the video camera stationed in the room would pick up the movement.

Our little threesome moved on to the next room newly energized, hoping the unusual activity would continue. That would not be the case, unfortunately.

On our third rotation, Wendy, Karen, and I were assigned to the playhouse. Deana and Kat were sent to the third floor.

For Kat and Deana, their time upstairs was relatively quiet and uneventful until 12:15 A.M. Deana lay on the bed while Kat sat in a nearby chair in one of the bedrooms. They were quietly observing the area when footsteps were heard.

At first, Deana thought it may have been Chris Cloud, MPI's tech manager, coming upstairs to check the video equipment. He did not appear. In the next instant, a bang similar to a cupboard door being firmly shut was clearly heard.

Deana sat up, "What was that?"

Together, they went out to check the living area, where the sound appeared to originate. The women examined the room, checking cupboards, windows, and doors. Each was securely closed as they had been since Deana and Kat's arrival.

Around: 12:22 A.M. Kat asked, "If someone is here with us, just give us a sign. Push the beds; knock on a wall." Shortly after, a light tap is heard. (The video clips for this can be viewed on our Web site's Secret Room.)

Later, based on MPI's detailed schedule, it was confirmed their tech manager, Chris, was nowhere near the third floor at the sound of the thumps. The source for this noise remains unexplained.

While that was going on in the house, the trio of Wendy, Karen, and I were in the little playhouse. Only there for a short time, I became really nervous and had to leave. I thought it was probably the two spiders we saw or maybe just the fact that the cabin was small and dark.

Karen and Wendy in the playhouse

Whatever the case, I headed outside to the protests of Wendy and Karen. Ten minutes later they came out to see what I was doing, or to get away from the spiders... hard to say. Anyway, I was just as uncomfortable outside as I was in the cabin and had to go in the house. It was as if something was drawing me back inside, some uncontrollable urge.

I went in and sat quietly in the dining room so as not to disturb the teams investigating throughout the house. Sitting in a frozen position for over an hour was a little uncomfortable. I didn't want to turn up as an EVP on someone's recorder. Even so, just being inside made me feel much better and more relaxed.

The evening continued without any other noteworthy event. Around 3:30 A.M. Chris and Wayne said to wrap it up. The MPI team went to work as we bid farewell to Julie. Even though I hated to leave, we were exhausted and had to get some rest. She was excited and eager to learn what had been discovered. There were hours of video and audio recordings and hundreds of photographs to review. This would take several weeks to accurately complete. Little did we know our

Deana and Chris go over some evidence

adventure into the paranormal had just begun.

We arrived at the office late the next morning. One of the first e-mails in our box was from Liz, a descendant of the Wallace family. She left us a phone number if we wanted to chat about the Wallace family. Without hesitation, Kat picked up the phone and called. Her story was an interesting one.

When Kat first told her about the possible paranormal activity at the Wallace's Bay Port home, Liz chuckled and said, "I'm not surprised. Tragedy and mystery has followed my family for decades." It seemed many of her ancestors died at an early age from accidents or sudden, tragic illness."

Kat listened intently as she unraveled the early years of the Wallace family. From what Liz knew, William was a loving, devoted father and husband. William and his first wife were married for seven years and had five children.

Liz had very little additional information on William's first marriage. She thought his wife's name was either Frances or Elizabeth but wasn't certain. The family archives had many photographs dating back more than a hundred years. Strangely, Liz said, there was not one photograph of Frances.

Through the family, she had heard that Frances was a kind and devoted mother and wife, gentle in nature with a good sense of humor. William and their children loved her dearly. The exact cause for Frances' sudden death, at the young age of twenty-seven, was unknown.

Liz continued her family story, telling us that William remarried about a year after his first wife's death to a woman called Margaret. It is written in letters that the marriage "...was one of love, not necessity."

Margaret was a very different sort of woman than William's first wife. While Frances was a gentle soul with a good sense of humor, Margaret was rather conservative and somewhat strict. Letters Margaret wrote to family indicate she was having a rather difficult time adjusting to William's children, Nellie, Belle, Robert, Frances, and William Jr. (Billy). They, in turn, had a problem seeing her as their real mother. It was a stressful period for everyone.

Liz went on to tell us about the family's favorite wild child, Ora. Ora was the daughter of Margaret and William. It seems fate wasn't on Margaret's side when such a conservative woman would give birth to a stubborn, independent, uncontrollable, and party-loving daughter.

In fact, to prevent Ora from gallivanting with friends, Margaret would sometimes lock her on the third floor. Ora would have tantrums, slamming doors and throwing things about. This

Margaret Wallace and the Wallace children

determined young woman could not be contained. She discovered a drainpipe by a third-floor window that she would climb down to meet friends and climb up before her mother knew she was gone.

It seems that through these difficult years it was Belle who was the family mediator. Belle was very much like her mother, Frances. Warm, loving, patient, she watched over and cared for the younger children. In fact, all the Wallace children adored Belle and relied on her for many things. She was always there for them… always.

When Ora grew up, her partying ways turned into full-fledged alcoholism. She was sent to sanitariums on occasions to "dry out." During those times, Belle always found a place to stay nearby to support Ora's progress. Sadly, even with Belle's support, alcoholism was the master, and Ora died while still in her twenties.

Further tragedies befell the Wallace clan. Belle's youngest sister, Frances, died from a burst appendix while at prep school. William's second wife, Margaret, died suddenly while packing to vacation at their Bay Port summer home, and William died in a car accident. Strangely, a newspaper article mentioned he was expected to fully recover from his injuries. The next day, however, the same newspaper told of his death.

We had successfully gathered all this information on the Wallace family but still found nothing on William's first wife. What had happened to her? Why was there so little information known about her death?

Our research on the Wallace family hit a wall, and we had to turn to outside help. Fortunately, we found a dedicated Huron County historian, Diana Hebner. After days of researching historical records, she found out what happened to Frances.

An April 14, 1893 front page article in the *Huron Tribune*, began, "The death of Mrs. William H. Wallace, at Bay Port, on Wednesday night is an event of peculiar sadness." Indeed, the story that follows is both bizarre and mysterious.

One morning Frances woke up and found a small pimple on her chin. She scratched it and thought nothing more. On Saturday, a few days later, she went to the dentist and had a tooth extracted. By evening, "…the pimple had become a painful sore."

It rapidly became infected, and blood poisoning set in. Three doctors were brought in to consult. Nothing they did would be enough to save her. According to the article, "...her system did not possess the vital force to rally after the poisoning had been controlled...." At 9:45 P.M., Wednesday evening, Frances died.

The story doesn't end there. "On Monday, though none else were alarmed, she [Frances] seemed to have a premonition of her approaching end and told her husband and aunt that she did not fear to die, that she was ready to go."

After her death, Frances was laid out in the Bay Port home. On the day of her funeral, a special train stopped at the home to take her remains to Port Austin for final burial.

As I sat back and contemplated all that happened to the Wallace family in their Bay Port home, some things became clear. Within six months of Frances giving birth to little Billy, she developed a deadly infection. In a very weakened state, the infection could not be controlled.

During that period in America, it was common for births as well as illnesses to be treated in the home. During Frances' pregnancy and tragic illness, she was at home. It seems likely Mr. Wallace sent the children outside so they would not hear Frances' painful cries. He may also have sent them outside to keep them out of the way of doctors and nurses.

Perhaps the reported paranormal activity in the Rose Room was related to the quick and horrific death of the children's mother, Frances. When Julie's daughter and friend were in the playhouse, they heard screams of a woman. Is it possible they picked up the residual energy of the Wallace children who had stood in the yard listening to the cries of their mother?

Could the unexplainable bangs and the thumps be related to Ora's tantrums when her mother locked her on the third floor? It might also be the sound of Ora sneaking in and out of the window to meet her friends.

After days of evidence review, the MPI team did not come up with any evidence to indicate paranormal activity in the home. The cameras were not positioned properly to see the moving lace on the canopy bed. Only the steps heard on the third floor and the thump were recorded (you can hear that in our Secret Room).

Now comes a truly unexpected turn. Something we would never have anticipated. It started when Wallace descendants sent us family photographs. Reviewing the assortment of pictures, Kat came across photos of the children, and something struck her as familiar. Belle, Frances' second oldest daughter, looked like someone Kat had seen before. She showed it to me. Oddly enough, it looked like someone I'd seen as well.

We began shuffling through stacks of old photographs and stopped at one in absolute amazement. In this story you'll see the photograph of Belle we pulled out from the Wallace family portrait. Below (left) you'll see the photograph of Belle. Next to it (right) is the photograph of a young girl taken seventy years later. The young girl in the more recent photograph is no relation to the Wallace family, but we noticed a strong resemblance. Do you? You can check our Web site's Secret Room to see the facial transition in slow motion to help you clearly see the similarity.

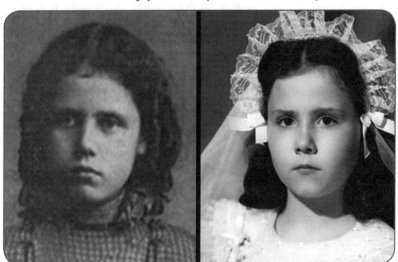

Photograph on left Courtesy of Liz Montgomery, Wallace family descendant

Startling similarities between these two children

The young girl in the more recent photograph has grown up. Now, you're probably wondering who this young girl is. It's me.

How could this be? I'm not related to the Wallace family. In fact, my ancestry is not even Scottish/English. Recalling my experience at Sweet Dreams Inn Victorian Bed and Breakfast, I began to wonder if it was actually possible that there was some kind of fateful, spiritual reconnection.

At first sight, the home had pulled me to it. There was a strong feeling of déjà vu I had never experienced before or since. When we arrived, I knew exactly how the home's interior was laid out, like I'd been there before.

The first time I saw the third floor, I expected it to be more open. Julie explained that it had originally been one large room but later divided into smaller rooms.

Did mere coincidence or something else cause the lace on the canopy bed to move when I called out the children's names? Also, that evening I didn't want to be outside. While in the log cabin and then standing in the yard I was compelled to go back in the house. Was it to be closer to Frances as she was giving birth to Billy or possibly while dying from the infection?

It seems that I (or Belle) was drawn back to the Bay Port home. Could unfinished business have brought Belle home? Perhaps Frances or the children needed to see Belle once more. It is uncertain. This I do know. I want to go back. I *need* to go back. Something continues to draw me there. Perhaps on my next visit I'll know.

Story Five
The Indigo Inn and Down and Under Lounge and Grille

Original DaHaas Hotel, Circa 1888

Fremont, Michigan
Web site: www.HauntedTravelsMI.com
Secret Room Password: f263m
Paranormal Teams:
Michigan's Otherside and
Organization for the Research
and Science of the Paranormal (ORSP)

Our first spring trip after a grueling Michigan winter was to the historic Indigo Inn in Fremont, which is a little town north of Grand Rapids. Built in the 1800s, the inn has a colorful history with a reputation for being haunted. The current owner, Marilyn Heeringa, has given new life to this historic hotel. Over the past couple of years, she has literally redone all the rooms, from top to bottom. We were eager to see what Marilyn had accomplished and if stories of the haunting were true.

On this investigation we would be meeting up with Tom Maat and Amberrose Hammond from Michigan's Otherside. Tom and Amberrose are one of Michigan's most highly respected investigative duos. Ivan Tunney from Organization for the Research and Science of the Paranormal (ORSP) would be joining the investigation. Dan Brunner, a very gifted sensitive Ivan enlisted on a previous investigation would also be joining the group.

We took off on a bright sunny morning. By early afternoon, dark storm clouds drifted past the sun. They were not pretty. It started to snow. Within minutes, more than an inch had fallen and there was no sign that the storm would subside. As it turned out, this would be one of Michigan's biggest Nor'easters. Because of the weather, only Tom Maat and Dan Brunner were able to complete

The Indigo Inn, 2008

the trip. Though our team was a bit smaller than expected, we were no less eager or able for this investigation.

Bev and I were the first to arrive and easily found the inn, which is located in the heart of Fremont. Indigo's brick front has changed little over the decades and clearly retains its old-world look.

Entering, we were pleasantly surprised at the charming interior. To the right is the Indigo Wireless Café and Tea Room, which was especially appealing on this cold, blustery day. The Brass Wind Gallery, a delightful little gift shop featuring works of area artisans, is on the left. Sheree Lincoln and her husband own and operate the little shop.

Indigo Café and Tea Room

The Brass Wind Gallery

Sheree is also the web designer and is the marketing consultant for Marilyn Heeringa. She sometimes helps Marilyn with the inn while she's away. Sheree greeted us with a warm welcome and took us to our rooms on the second floor.

Sheree explained that Marilyn, when renovating the bed and breakfast, wanted to keep its turn-of-the-century atmosphere. We were impressed with the quality and beauty of the restoration. Four rooms are located just off the second-floor landing. These rooms

offer private baths.
The remaining four
rooms share a single,
small bathroom with
a shower at the end
of the hall. Of course,
the bathroom and
fixtures have all been
updated, but you
certainly get a sense
of what it was like in
the early days.

Small, but warm and inviting bedroom

All rooms are newly decorated with light, cheerful colors and floral touches. The four hallway rooms are definitely smaller, with limited space, but the beds are welcoming and very comfortable.

Once settled, we rejoined Sheree in her gift shop. Before heading off to dinner, she filled us in on some of the history.

The inn was originally built sometime in the late 1800s. Named after its first owner, John DeHaas, the DeHaas House Hotel quickly grew to prominence as Fremont's finest accommodation. In 1887, it was destroyed by fire. Not to be deterred, John rebuilt his lodging bigger and grander than the first. The new design resembled a classic English pub and inn with a spacious lobby on the main floor. The hotel also housed a dining room, saloon, barbershop, and pool hall making it a center of activity for the area.

Over the years, the hotel hosted many prominent business leaders and political figures including the governor and lieutenant governor of Michigan. In 1923, the Fremont State Bank bought the hotel and tore it down. Coincidently, John DeHaas died that same year. In 1924, the bank, along with a business consortium, erected a new hotel, the Kimbark Inn. Now things get a little more colorful.

Apparently, this prominent hotel hosted more than just well-known business leaders. Sheree told us it also served as a bordello. She believes the bordello started around the turn of the century and ran its profitable operations through, at least, the 1930s. It seems that some of the prominent business and political leaders, along with lonely travelers, found this particular activity another enticing feature of the hotel.

Kimbark Inn, circa 1925

The Prohibition Era of the 1920s were crazy times at the Kimbark. During that period, we're told the hotel housed a speakeasy and served bootlegged liquor to its select customers. Al Capone frequented the area, and the Kimbark was one of his stops.

For those who don't know, liquor was banned in the 1920s. Speakeasies (illegal, underground bars and nightclubs) began around the 1890s, but their heyday was the prohibition period of the 1920s through the early 1930s.

The term *speakeasy* was tagged because patrons were asked to be very discrete about who they told about the place in order to keep it secret from the authorities. In other words, people frequenting these places were asked to "speak easy."

When prohibition ended, things quieted down at the Kimbark. In 1951 Mr. and Mrs. P.A.C. McIntyre purchased and operated the hotel. Mr. McIntyre died in 1957 and, two years later, Mrs. McIntyre sold the property. The years that followed were not kind to the hotel, which turned into a flophouse in the 1970s. Back then, it became a frequent hangout for drifters, drug dealers, drunks, and bums.

As Sheree came to the end of her story, the phone rang. It was Tom. The weather was delaying his arrival. We expected Dan would also be delayed, so we asked Sheree to go ahead and give us the tour.

She took us back to the second floor. The hallway leading to the smaller rooms had reports of a little girl's presence. This was seen on many occasions along with the dark shadow of a woman gazing out the window.

Continuing, we noted two doors closed on both ends of the second floor. Sheree mentioned they were areas being renovated for office space. In these sections of the building, however, people had seen a dark, menacing figure.

More reports of paranormal activity come from the Down and Under Lounge and Grille, located just below the inn. Shadows of women are seen in the hall vanishing through a storage

The spirit of a little girl is frequently seen in the hallway

room door. This room was once the entrance to a stairway leading upstairs. It is thought these ghostly figures may be the apparitions of prostitutes that once frequented the hotel. Could these ladies still be looking for business?

Sheree added that several other strange events happened at the bar. Marjorie Phillips, manager of the bar and Marilyn's business partner, would explain later.

Sheree came to the end of the tour. With a long evening ahead, we thought it was about time to take a little dinner break. Sheree was meeting her husband and some friends at a local restaurant and invited us along. We were very happy to accept. Her phone rang again. Tom was still some distance away. Sheree mentioned we were having dinner. Tom said if it weren't too late he'd meet us there.

Fortunately, the brunt of the storm was staying just south of Fremont so the roads weren't too treacherous. The restaurant Sheree took us to was a friendly little place next to Fremont's golf course.

Swirling snowflakes and the night sky obscured the view of the scenic grounds from the wall of windows. On a beautiful summer day, however, we could imagine the sight would be awesome.

We shared warm conversation and a delicious meal with our group of six as the winter storm raged outside. Sheree, Bev, and I were relieved when Tom finally arrived safe from the hazardous trip. He came in looking very much like a snowman but with a big smile on his face. He sat down and said, "I'm a Michigan man. Weather doesn't bother me."

We finished our dinners and conversation. Saying our goodbyes, we headed back to the inn. In our absence, Dan had arrived but left for a quick dinner. Within a short time he was back, looking relaxed and ready to go.

Having previously visited the inn, Tom was familiar with its layout and active areas. Even so, before he set up equipment, he thought Dan should go through the building to pick up on current energies for this investigation.

Tom Maat, setting up equipment

The group followed Dan to the second floor. He stopped half way up the stairway and gazed at the painting on the wall. A little ballerina, perhaps ten years old, looked back. She wore a long lace dress and ballerina shoes. Her image was clearly turn-of-the century.

This slender young child with curly, light brown hair wore an elfish smile as if mischievous thoughts were racing through her mind. Dan asked if this was the little girl whose spirit remained in the house. We said no but may have been wrong. Marilyn would later tell us about her unusual compulsion to buy the painting and place it where she did. Several guests and a few psychics have told her the child apparition they had seen looked very much like the little girl in the painting.

Entering the second floor, Dan sensed a considerable amount of residual spirit energy around the main landing. Moving to the opposite hall with the smaller rooms, he detected even more residual energy. He felt guests would frequently see shadows from the corner of their eye. This was, in fact, the area where apparitions of a little girl and a woman staring out the window have been seen on several occasions.

Portrait courtesy of the Indigo Inn

Is this the portrait of the little girl spirit?

We followed Dan to the end of the hall. He walked to the room that was Tom's and opened it. Tom stood briefly in amazement. "That's neat," he said. "I locked that. It's interesting that it just opened. I tested the lock."

Dan shook his head as he exited the room. "I can't say… it's just full. It's like every room. There's something in every friggin' room." He claimed many layers of spiritual energy were overwhelming his senses.

Next, he went into Marilyn's private suite of rooms not knowing they belonged to her. He didn't like many of the Egyptian artifacts she had displayed. Dan picked up a bad energy from them. Tom agreed saying, "You just get that oppressive feeling."

Leaving Marilyn's room, we crossed the upper floor landing and Sheree unlocked the doors to the sealed portion of the building. The warmth of the inn suddenly slipped away. Our flashlights gave us a narrow path of light in the corridor's darkness.

Here, renovations were beginning to convert the Kimbark's old apartments into office space. Dust clouded the air as we moved into the unlit interior. Cracked walls and chipped paint mingled with the smell of new construction.

Dark hallway where shadows are frequently seen

We noticed an immediate change in Dan. He began to move quickly and talk in rapid, short sentences.

"There's a shadow person… in the hallway right there. I think you'll see him walking across." Dan couldn't be sure if it was male or female.

Tom mentioned, during a previous visit, the psychic with him saw something similar. At that time, the shadow was identified as a tall, thin man. Tom said, "She actually had visualized a very tall man… standing in the doorway."

Entering another room, Dan stood for a moment. "Who's McIntyre?" Dan wasn't able to pick up anything on him, only that he was somehow connected to the hotel. We all looked at him in surprise. Sheree told Bev and I earlier P.A.C. McIntyre and his wife owned the hotel in the 1950s.

When the walk-through was complete, Tom and Dan decided to place cameras on the second floor to cover the main landing and stairway. I also placed my audio recorder on a table leading to the hallway where the little girl's spirit and shadows down the hall had been heard and seen. Additional cameras and audio recorders were placed in the corridor where the shadow person was seen.

Just about that time, Marilyn returned to the inn from an expo she had attended. Marilyn is an incredibly interesting woman who has traveled throughout the world. Though experienced and worldly, she is no less down-to-earth and friendly. We sat as she told us more about her inn.

It was a grand place, she said. "They had a lot of important dignitaries, and people with a lot of influence came through here… it's all documented." In fact, the inn's current café was once a grand ballroom for dancing and elegant events. The inn was quite a showplace in its earlier days.

Marilyn Heeringa
with her little helper, Precious

When Marilyn purchased the hotel, it was in terrible condition. She decided to restore it to its original quality. "If you wanted to make it grand you had to really do something nice to it," Marilyn said. "So that's when I started working on it and doing what I needed to do."

Marilyn is pleased with the results and particularly fascinated by the hotel's history. She has collected and maintains a large historical file.

As far as the history of the haunting, Marilyn recalls a conversation with an elderly man somewhere in his eighties. He was once a bellboy and busboy at the old hotel. He told her emphatically, "You know this place is haunted!"

Marilyn said she was not surprised, though personally she never had any encounters. She went on to tell us, however, that many others had.

During renovation of the inn, workers wouldn't stay after six o'clock. They claimed their tools were moved, and they would hear noises and voices on the main landing of the second level.

While construction was going on, a friend of Marilyn's stayed in one of the second floor rooms for a night. When Marilyn came back the next morning, he said, "Man there's a lot of activity going on… there was walking and clanging, shutting doors and talking." Her friend was so spooked he refused to stay on the second floor again.

She also mentioned others had seen the ghosts of a woman and little girl. One particular account was from a woman who came to the restaurant with her granddaughter. Marilyn invited them to sit at a particular table. The younger woman told her they would prefer to eat at another.

Later, the young woman came up to Marilyn, "I didn't mean to be rude, but that table was taken."

"Oh really?" Marilyn said.

"Yeah, there was a lady and her little daughter sitting there, and I didn't want to disturb them." Marilyn was a little surprised because she had seen no one.

She then introduced us to her business partner, Marjorie Phillips. Marjorie had quite a few experiences at both the inn and bar. As Tom, Dan, and Bev began the investigation, Marilyn and I sat down with Marjorie.

For more than eight years, Marjorie has experienced unusual phenomena in both the lounge and inn. In fact, she feels her senses are becoming more in-tune to the spirits, and they frequently communicate with her. The lounge has been very active with shadow people being seen, voices heard, and objects moving inexplicably.

The dark apparition of a man is often seen in the

Marjorie Phillips talks about her haunting experiences

bar. Marjorie described him. "He was dark... very thin and tall, very, very tall with a tall hat." He was so tall, in fact, he had to stoop down to pass through the doorway.

As many others had sensed, Marjorie also sees the spirits of a woman and little girl at the inn. She believes the name of the woman is Elizabeth and the little girl is Carolyn. The woman and child lived at the inn and died in a buggy accident.

Marjorie went on to tell us about the two male spirits who reside in the closed sections of the building. A psychic who had previously visited said one of the spirits was a man by the name of Sam Simlow (Semlow) or Sam Simpson. Marjorie believes he may have died in the 1887 fire.

We located an 1870 and 1880 census which showed a Sam Simpson lived in Kalamazoo. This would put him about ninety-five miles from the town of Fremont. There was also a Semlow family living in Fremont. One of the Semlows was nicknamed "Sem." There were no Simpson, Semlow, or Simlow deaths we were able to find during the late 1880s.

The other male presence is Frank. Marjorie believes he ran the hotel. Frank was a mean, domineering, controlling, and strong-willed person. Though Marjorie does not know how Frank died, she senses it was a violent death. Today, his spirit remains. He does not want to leave nor will he let the other spirits leave. Marjorie believes Frank was somehow connected or related to Elizabeth and Carolyn.

We found no one with the first name of Frank who owned or managed the hotel. There was, however, a Howard F. (Frank) Heldenbrand who ran the hotel in the 1920s. Howard did have a daughter named Elizabeth. Beyond that, we can make no connection. There is no record of an "Elizabeth" or "Carolyn" dying in a car or buggy accident.

Later, after the bar closed, we would be heading to the lounge to investigate possible activity. For now, however, we re-joined the group.

While Bev chatted with Tom, Sheree, and Marilyn, I followed Dan and Marjorie as they explored the first floor. We crowded into a small, dark hallway behind the kitchen. I could tell Dan sensed something as he approached a door located under the stairs. He opened it and looked inside then quickly retreated.

"I don't know what's in there, but I don't like it. I'm going to shut the door. I don't want it open."

"What do you sense in there?" I asked.

Dan shook his head, "I don't know what it is, but I don't like it."

I squeezed passed him. "I'm going to look."

"Go ahead," he replied as he moved pass me into the kitchen.

I opened the door and walked into the pitch-black interior of the small room. I flipped on my flashlight. There was nothing unusual. It looked and felt pretty much like your basic pantry/ storage room. Backing out, I turned to find Dan in the hallway behind me. He looked a little concerned and urged me to get out.

Retreating to the kitchen, I asked Marjorie, "What's in there?"

"It's Frank," she replied. "He's all over."

Later that evening, Sheree, Dan, Bev, and I were talking in the gift shop. We smelled an unusually pungent odor and turned to see Tom walk in with burning sage. We asked him what was up. Something very powerful and negative had surrounded him in the pantry/storage room. Tom was using the sage to clear the bad spirits. His reaction to the little room was even stronger than Dan's.

Tom explained that he looked up and saw something near the ceiling. "There you are!"

At that moment, he felt smoke began to swirl around him. The smoke was behaving like a vortex or spinning energy. Some believe a vortex is a doorway to the other side.

Tom continued, "You know the feeling you get when you're falling? I stopped... I just felt like I was going to fall into a black hole. That's what it felt like. The old fight or flight kicked in. That's when I said, okay, I'm coming back with some sage. I'm going to clear myself. This is one of those things where you decide if it's worth getting into a confrontation or just leave it alone."

The feelings Dan and Tom had in that storage room were intensely negative. They were faced with a difficult decision. Dan did not want to go back in, and Tom didn't want to confront it by himself. The pantry/storage room was not mentioned again that evening.

Returning to the second floor, Dan, Bev, and I turned left to go to the other wing, also under construction. Just like the section on the right, there was no electricity. Flashlights were our lifelines.

We followed a path to the *black room*, found at the end of the hall. We were at this

Dan senses negative energy in the oppressive "Black Room"

location earlier in the evening. Its very atmosphere was unsettling. At some point in time, someone painted the room completely black. Portions were still black. The room actually did create a feeling of intense heaviness. It was almost hard to breathe.

We were approaching the room when Dan called to us, "Something just shot in here." We quickly joined him. He scanned the room and continued, "This whole room is negative... heavy."

Dan again saw the shadow. It had swept into a dark corner of the room. I turned my video camera in that direction... nothing. Our video and audio recorders continued to run as we conducted a brief EVP session. We lingered for quite a while but nothing happened.

Eventually, we went back to the gift shop. Time was spent talking about the night's happenings and taking several stunning group photos. It's remarkable how attractive people are at 2:00 in the morning. Around 2:45 A.M. the music from the downstairs bar stopped, signaling its closing. The final stage of our investigation could begin. We headed downstairs.

The Down and Under Lounge and Grille is a laid-back, fun place great for karaoke, pool, or just to hang out with friends for a few drinks. It features live entertainment. One of the best parts of the Down and Under is the friendly staff. This great group of people loves the work and keeps the bar's energy level upbeat and fun.

We talked with a few of the bar's employees, Nadine Andrews and Julie Lowery. Each had witnessed paranormal events over the years.

Sheree Lincoln, Tom Maat, and Dan Brunner

For Nadine, there was one particular incident that stood out in her mind. She told us the story.

"On a Friday night we had an entertainer down here… she was a one-person show. She had a couple of different instruments. She had a guitar, and it was sitting on a stand. It [the guitar] was sitting about four feet away. There was nothing around that could have disturbed that stand. Just as she was getting ready to start playing a song, the guitar… literally came up off the stand and crashed

The Down and Under Bar and Grille

to the floor. It did quite a bit of damage to the guitar. Everybody in the bar went silent. You could hear the guitar reverberating." Nadine mentioned that at least five of the customers saw it happen, and more than twenty people heard it.

Julie shared one of her most recent experiences. It had occurred one afternoon as she was entering the front doors of the inn. As Julie tells us, "Just as I got into the front door, I heard a man shout, *'Get the hell out of here!'*" She shook her head and laughed, "There were no men in the building." Julie continued, "There have been other times we've been down here [Down and Under] when we've heard a name called out."

I thanked the women for their time and stories. Marjorie then took us back to the storage room to show us the hidden door we had heard about earlier in the evening. This was said to have been the secret entrance and exit for the men and women who used the bordello. The stairs have been removed and the door boarded off for many years. You can, however, still see the markings. There are many sightings of women and shadows passing through the hallway into the storage room. Many believe they are spirits of the ladies of the night and their customers.

After the interviews were complete, equipment was quickly set in the main bar and pool room. One camera was focused on a drinking glass that had been placed in the center of a table. This would be a test object in the hopes of recording its movement.

Time passed quietly. The glass everyone had been watching for the better part of an hour never moved. It was a little after 4:00 A.M. Tom called it a wrap. It had been an interesting but very long day. We were happy to head up to our rooms.

The next morning, after a delicious breakfast freshly prepared by Marilyn, we said our goodbyes and headed back. We wondered what the hours of recorded material would reveal.

A few days later, Tom and Amberrose called. Their video and photographs had revealed nothing, but they had captured one EVP. They would e-mail it the next morning. Since nothing had turned up on our video and audio recordings so far, we were excited to learn they may have gotten something.

(L to R) Kat, Dan, Tom, Bev

The next morning we downloaded the audio clip. It was captured on the second floor landing around 10:40 P.M. We were walking down the corridor when Dan said he was feeling residual energy everywhere. There it was, a very faint voice whispered, "Ghosts." Even though the word was soft, it was remarkably clear.

After that, Bev and I continued our evidence review with renewed interest. The minutes dragged to hours. My fingers were going into the air guitar position for a little imaginary rock concert. Bev was sleeping in the chair next to me… she wouldn't notice I was having a private concert. My guitar solo stopped. I had heard something.

This EVP was recorded at the time Dan, Bev, and I were in the black room. Dan had seen a shadow and called us to the room saying, "Something just shot in there."

After we joined Dan, I asked, "Is somebody in here? Let us know." There it was. The decibels were very low. I adjusted the sound. A soft male voice whispered, "Bright boy." Perhaps it was a response to Dan's earlier comment. At least, I hoped it was responding to Dan. I secretly prayed it wasn't referring to me! If it were, I would have to start thinking of doing something different with my hair or, perhaps, start wearing more dresses.

In any event, I must admit I got a little excited. I reached over to tap Bev awake. Maybe the tap was a little stronger than I had intended. Bev jumped up and began speaking a whole new language. Was she channeling? Hmmm, I think not. I pulled her down from the ceiling, apologized, and then explained why I was so excited.

We now began to pay very close attention as we meticulously went over all of the audio and video. More EVPs began to emerge. Most of them occurred between 1:00 A.M. to 2:15 A.M. while Dan, Bev, and I were in the black room and corridor. Some of the more audible EVPs were male voices. It was difficult to tell if the EVPs were the same voice or different.

One seemed to say, "Very odd." Another was heard in a different location in the dark hallway after I had again asked the question, "Is somebody in here?" We're uncertain what this EVP says. There are varying interpretations. Some believe it says, "Why are we here? Tell me." Others think it's, "Do we harm? Tell me." Another interpretation is, "We hear… tell me." The final EVP was a male voice that whispered, "I am alone."

Probably the most unsettling EVP was recorded near the grandfather clock on the second floor landing. It was around 2:35 A.M. No one was in the area at the time. Most of the audio sequence is white noise except for the ticking of the clock. The EVP recorded sounds very much like a child's voice. Two words are heard, "It's scary."

Interestingly, this is the same location where a little girl's apparition is seen and heard by staff and guests. This audio clip and others can be seen and heard in our Web site's Secret Room.

The amazing history of the Indigo Inn naturally lends itself to ghost stories. Certainly, many older or historic buildings have ghost stories attached to them. Are they real or just a collection of stories and active minds?

Unfortunately, we had no personal experiences during our visit. Based on the number of recorded voice phenomena and the experiences of Tom, Dan, the staff, and some patrons, we do believe something unusual or paranormal may be going on at the Indigo. For those interested in the paranormal, it will be fun to spend the night and find out.

An EVP was collected near the grandfather clock

Story Six
John A. Lau Saloon

John Lau in his saloon, circa 1890

Alpena, Michigan
Web site: www.HauntedTravelsMI.com
Secret Room Password: bjr48
Paranormal Investigative Team:
Mid Michigan Paranormal Investigators

Alpena was a rough-and-tumble northeastern Michigan town in 1870's America. Forests covered this sparsely populated land located along the shores of Lake Huron's Thunder Bay. Lumberjacks and longshoremen were pretty much the only jobs around. Small businesses popped up to provide supplies, food, and liquor to this rugged group of people. A resourceful, young German immigrant by the name of John A. Lau decided he'd supply the liquor and in the late 1800s opened the John A. Lau Saloon.

In June 1900, John married Agnes Paddock and together grew their business and a family. John and Agnes had five children, only three lived. John, Alfred, and little Madelyn.

Little is known about John and Agnes Lau. We did find that Agnes had been ill for some time. Even as the illness progressed, she continued to work at the saloon. Eventually, it became too much for her. In the fall of 1912, she went to live in Detroit with her mother, Mrs. Paddock. There she would receive special medical treatments. It didn't help. Her health continued to decline over the winter, and she finally died on July 24, 1913.

It is believed she passed away from consumption (TB). That seems possible since it was a very common illness in those days. During Agnes' steady decline, John was very concerned for her. In fact, he and the children spent most of their time with Agnes in Detroit. From an article dated July 24, 1913, in the *Alpena News*, "He [John] was at her bedside when the end came."

After Agnes' death, it was suggested the children should be sent to an orphanage in Detroit. We could find no information to indicate this ever happened.

Thanks to the dedication of a local historian, Diana Hebner, we gathered more information about the family. Based on the 1920 census, we do know that their oldest son, John, was living with the Paddocks (Agnes' family) in Detroit. He worked at the newspaper. Alfred and Madelyn were living with their father in Alpena.

On March 11, 1922, John A. Lau, at the age of fifty-six, would join his wife in death. He had been ill for some time with heart disease. Three weeks prior to his death he suffered a heart attack and was confined to his bed. He died at his residence in the saloon.

John was laid out next-door at Owen Funeral Parlor, now a part of the restaurant. Both John and Agnes are buried in Alpena.

John and Agnes loved the saloon and the little town of Alpena. Their business rapidly grew, as did the town. As mentioned earlier, the men in this community worked hard, drank hard, and fought hard. Liquor and anger are evil companions, and the saloon saw plenty of both. Skirmishes were frequent.

One of the most notable fights made the headlines of the *Alpena Evening News*, July 29 and 30, 1913. It started when Frank Prena, a longshoreman, had just a little too much to drink and got into an argument with another patron. As the argument got louder and more violent, Prena was ready to attack the other man. Fred Kraemer stepped in and tried to break up the fight. Prena pulled out a knife and stabbed him three times in the abdomen and lower hip.

Blood pulsed from his body. Clutching his wounds, Kraemer left the saloon staggering to the doctor's office. A growing crowd followed him, though no one attempted to help. The doctor's office was closed. Confused and in shock, Kraemer went back to the bar and collapsed on the floor. He was finally taken to a doctor for care.

While this was going on, a drunk and frightened Prena ran home with the police in hot pursuit. After a violent struggle, they brought him to the ground and cuffed him. He was booked on assault to do great bodily harm and jailed pending trial. When Prena was taken to the cellblock in the county jail, he passed his son, also in prison on a minor charge. Seeing his father pass by, he gave a sneering laugh.

We don't know what happened to Kraemer. The July 29 article seemed to indicate he would recover. The next day, however, the newspaper said his chances of recovery were, "considered doubtful." We were not able to find any further information on him.

After John A. Lau's death, the saloon remained a popular place. Apartments were added on the second floor at some point in the building's history. The saloon and apartments eventually closed, remaining vacant and neglected for years. In 1987, the new owners took over and began restoration.

Today, many people believe it is Agnes' spirit haunting the restaurant. She seems to be protective of the saloon and employees. If she doesn't like a new employee, they're in trouble. She has been known to throw things and make employees drop their trays or misplace things. Agnes also has a softer side. When an employee is sad or troubled, they just may feel a pat on the back or little squeeze from the motherly spirit. According to Mid Michigan Paranormal Investigators, restaurant customers and employees have seen a woman move up the stairs, felt cold spots, and smelled unusual odors.

Most things seem to point to Agnes, but is she the only spirit roaming? Could the violence of its past remain? Perhaps Prena's anger lingers. It might even be the ghost of a favorite patron. Of course, we can't forget about the Owens Funeral Parlor, which is now part of the restaurant. The haunting could be from one of its former customers. We hoped to find out during this investigation.

We first learned of the haunting through Matt and Melanie Moyer, co-founders of Mid Michigan Paranormal Investigators (MMPI). They had investigated the saloon on other occasions with some interesting results. When they invited us, we were very happy to accept.

It was a cool, crisp fall day, and Kat's husband, Chris, was joining us for the trip. Chris doesn't share our fascination with ghosting, but he thought the road trip might be fun, and the motel's heated in-door pool and hot tub sounded pretty good. We arrived early and settled into our rooms. Chris checked out the pool area. It looked great. Then it was off to the John A. Lau Saloon for some dinner.

From the life-sized model Indian nicknamed Indian Bob, to the lady in the bathtub and large moose head on the wall, the atmosphere is fun and funky. Yet, it hasn't lost its historical theme. Entering the restaurant, past Indian Bob, your attention is drawn to the bar that looks like it came out of the Old West. There is even the portrait of a naked lady hanging behind the bar in a gilt-edged picture frame. This is actually the original section of the saloon.

Just to the right of the entrance, the area that is now the restaurant's banquet room used to be Owen's Funeral Parlor. The basement is supposedly where the embalming took place more than a hundred years ago. Above the banquet room are now vacant rooms that used to be offices and apartments.

Round and square dark wood tables and chairs scattered in the bar and dining area should have gunslingers sitting, drinking whiskey, and playing poker. Instead, we saw a room filled with families and couples of all ages — just regular people wearing countless docker

Indian Bob

slacks with cell phones clipped at the waist. In the center of it all were two hungry ghostwriters and a husband.

Like the people inside, the restaurant's menu is diverse and casual. Sitting in the upper floor dining area reviewing the menu, we decided to order what a lumberjack would have selected. We made our decisions. Kat chose the Seabake Fettuccine, and I preferred the King Crab and Asparagus Salad. We turned to see what Chris was ordering and noticed what might have been considered a look of disgust.

"Are you kidding me? You really think a lumberjack would order a King Crab and Asparagus Salad!"

Chris pointed to the menu. "You order a burger or you order a steak, and it's got to be rare! Here, the Lumberjack Burger, that's what I am going to get. You should get the Old #7 Steak or the Hatchet Ribeye." He was treating, so we ordered his version of lumberjack food, except medium-well with a side salad. It was excellent.

After a leisurely dinner, we dropped Chris off at the motel. He was looking forward to a relaxing swim, time in the hot tub, and then a little basketball on TV.

Leaving the parking lot, we saw four school busses pull in filled with young boys. We wondered what was going on, but our attention was now on the investigation.

Returning to the restaurant, we met up with Matt, Melanie, and their team. They are a dedicated, down-to-earth group and very easy to work with. One of the things that drew us to MMPI was their scientific approach

Casual bar and restaurant setting

Matt Moyer giving last minute instructions to his members.

Melanie Moyer and crew setting up equipment

during investigations. They are very well equipped. MMPI uses voice recognition to help identify actual EVPs from the voices of team members.

Since MMPI conducted previous investigations at the saloon, they knew the most active locations and began setting up equipment. While the team was doing that, we spoke with Ed Sytek, the maintenance person. Over the past year, Ed experienced several unexplainable events.

One time, around 4:20 A.M., Ed was waxing the floor downstairs when he heard a door slam on the second level of the restaurant. He went up to investigate. There are only three doors up there. The owners had bolted one before they left earlier in the evening. The other two have automatic door closers making it impossible for them to slam. Ed couldn't account for the loud noise.

Ed Sytek talking about his personal experiences

Another time, he was mopping the floors when a glass fell off a shelf. The base and portion of the stem sat undisturbed on the counter. The top portion, however, literally shattered and flew across the hallway. Pieces were found all over the bar's floor.

Finishing up the interview, we thanked Ed and rejoined the group as Matt and Melanie gave assignments and final instructions. While I listened intently to what Matt was saying, Kat was focused on something else.

Her video camera running, she zoomed in on a small compass pinned to Matt's shirt. She interrupted briefly, "Matt, I have one question real quick. Is that your GPS system?"

Matt looked down at the compass and chuckled, "Electro magnetic fields interact with compasses. So, if we are in a place where we don't have the EMF with us and we are definitely feeling a presence, we will hold this up and shine our lights on it to see if it makes any kind of movement. It's kind of like dowsing rods… It's how you believe and what kinds of equipment you want to use." Matt continued to

Melanie and team member taking base readings

explain that their team likes to use all types of equipment from the more sophisticated to the basic during an investigation.

By 11:15 P.M. the customers were gone and it was time to begin the investigation. The group broke into two teams. EVP

Matt's team in an EVP session

sessions were conducted. The evening was moving along smoothly, though uneventfully, until Matt's team moved to the upper floor apartments.

No one is certain when the apartments were built. We were told Apartment 2 was used as an office by the Owen's Funeral Parlor. It's interesting to note that Apartment 2 is a location where Matt and Melanie had recorded some interesting EVPs during a previous investigation.

This area of the building was quite interesting and a definite contrast to the restaurant. While the first floor was beautifully maintained and restored to its 1870's ambiance, the rooms on the top floors had gone pretty much untouched for decades. The narrow stairway took us to a long, dark corridor without electricity or heat. In this gloomy part of the building, paint and plaster were peeling off walls. In a few spots, the floor had missing or broken boards. It would have made a great haunted house for Halloween.

Matt's group crowded into one unusually small room off of Apartment 2. It seemed even colder here than the rest of the floor. With recorders out, we started asking questions hoping for some ghostly response. During a pause, there came the faintest noise. We all spoke at once, "Did you hear that?"

It sounded like a low, deep growl that came above our heads, closer to the ceiling than the floor. This eerie noise was similar to an angry dog's growl just before the attack. It was unsettling. This happened three or four more times. Spaced a few minutes apart, they seemed random, not really responding to any specific questions. Since we were the only ones in the apartments, we wondered at its cause. Perhaps it was just an old building settling, or could it be something trying to reach us? Moving throughout the floor, we were hoping for more and were a little disappointed when nothing further happened. Hopefully, when reviewing evidence, something would turn up.

Meanwhile, Melanie's group and Kat were ending their uneventful investigation of the basement. Moving upstairs, they quietly headed to the balcony of the main restaurant.

On a previous visit, Frank, one of their team members, experienced an event while sitting at a table in this section. It felt like someone sat down next to him. Hoping to experience something similar, he sat at the same table.

Frank feels the table move

The group quietly chatted for a few minutes. It was then Kat noticed the battery in her camera was nearly drained.

"I need to recharge my battery," she said. "So I would like to go down…" Her words were cut short when Frank interrupted.

"Whoa… oh my God, this table just moved! I swear to God." All eyes turned to him.

Melanie calmly asked, "Are you bumping it?"

"No," he responded. "I am not. It moved." He looked a bit shaken.

Kat focused her video camera on the table, hoping the battery would hold out a little longer. The table remained perfectly still as the camera battery died.

The investigation continued as teams switched locations. Melanie's group moved up to the apartments while Matt's headed to the main restaurant.

The evening's chill had penetrated the upper floor. They could almost see their breath as the team quietly moved through the rooms.

Melanie set up the initial EVP session in the small room off Apartment 2. This is where Matt's team had heard the growl. Kat set her digital audio recorder on a table in the main section of the apartment before joining the others in the smaller room. After some time, the group wandered off into a back room to continue their silent vigil.

Melanie began asking questions. "You don't have to be shy. We're just here to visit." She briefly paused. "If you can use your voice, just come right up to the device in my hand and tell me your name."

Melanie's group in the apartments

"Did you hear that?" Frank said. "It sounded like it was below us." They had all heard the distant, metallic grinding noise.

There were no motors or electrical systems on the second floor that could possibly have made the noise. They wondered if it had come from downstairs, perhaps the first floor kitchen. Matt's team, stationed quietly on the first floor, heard nothing unusual.

It was a little after 3:00 A.M. when Matt and Melanie decided it was time to wrap up. As Melanie's team headed downstairs, Kat stopped in Apartment 2 to retrieve her audio recorder.

The evening's investigation had been interesting. We were optimistic about the possibility of getting some recorded evidence.

As equipment was being packed up, the group mentioned it was Melanie's birthday. They were taking her for a late snack to their favorite twenty-four-hour greasy spoon. What was Melanie's treat? Fries and gravy! As

Matt's team reviews EVP evidence

everybody told us, "Nothing is too good for our Melanie!" Melanie rolled her eyes in good fun.

Laughing, we said our goodbyes. Our time with Mat, Mel, and the MMPI folks had been very enjoyable. Gravy and fries were not in our future tonight... sleep was.

Arriving back at the motel, Kat quietly entered her room trying not to disturb Chris. She needn't have worried. A tornado blowing through the motel would not have disturbed him. Chris was definitely out for the count. Kat smiled. Nothing helps Chris sleep better than a good swim and relaxing hot tub.

The next morning I met them for breakfast. Kat, like myself, looked very tired. The big surprise was Chris. He seemed totally exhausted and worse than us. I said, "What's the matter Chris, didn't you sleep well?"

"I don't want to talk about it." He muttered as he studied the menu.

Kat chuckled. "Well, you remember those four busses we saw as we were leaving? They dropped off a hundred little ten-year-old hockey players. There was a state tournament this weekend. They invaded the pool while Chris was in there and spent all night screaming with excitement. He couldn't hear the game and couldn't sleep. He is not a happy camper this morning."

When I asked where the chaperones were, Chris glared at me. "They were all in my hot tub."

On the way home, Kat and I took turns driving because Chris was too tired. Occasionally, we'd hear him talking to himself. Kat said, "Don't pay any attention. Those are words he learned in the military."

Once again we found ourselves back in the office reviewing evidence. Experience told us it would take several long days to complete. Matt and Melanie had even more work ahead. During the investigation, they had set up numerous video cameras and audio recorders throughout the restaurant. They had countless hours of audio and video to review and analyze.

Over the next month, it was a joint effort of information sharing. They sent us audio clips with possible evidence, and we did the same. Matt and Melanie had also given us a CD with EVPs they collected during one of their past investigations at Lau.

Unfortunately, some evidence we were hoping to capture was not recorded, including the growl and the table movement. There were a few possible EVPs and a couple of unusual audio anomalies.

The first bit of evidence we collected was in the basement, recorded at approximately 11:22 P.M. Photographs were being taken and a few questions asked for possible EVP response. In between the questions, we captured a very soft male voice that says, "Come back for it." If you listen to this at our Web site, you will need to turn your sound up to hear it. The voice decibels are very low.

One EVP was collected in the basement

The next audio clips were not voices but unusual noises. The first came from Kat's audio recorder shortly after Frank thought he felt the table move. The recorder was placed on the upstairs table when this unusual noise occurred. It sounded a bit like a laser gun or some type of power interference. We're not sure what would have caused this since, at the time, no one had touched any power sources or machinery. This recorder was used on more than two dozen investigations over an eighteen-month period. It was the first time a sound like this was recorded.

The next noise was recorded around 2:08 A.M. in Apartment 2 on the top floor. This is the room where Kat left her digital audio recorder. Melanie's group was down the hall sitting in a back room. While there, they heard a faint metallic grinding noise like a generator or fan. Since there were no motors, heat, or even electricity on the top floor, the group thought it might be something from the floor below them. However, from the sound of the recording, the noise originated very closed to Kat's audio recorder. The cause remains unknown.

Without a doubt, the most compelling evidence came from MMPI during an investigation earlier in the year. Matt and Melanie do an amazing job cleaning up EVPs, and what they captured is incredible.

The first is remarkably clear. It seems to say, "Indian Bob." Strangely enough, that's the nickname given to the life-size model of an Indian sitting at the restaurant's entrance.

The next is just as clear. It's a woman's voice. According to MMPI, there were no women present when this was recorded. The last part of the recording clearly says, "Don't go." In the middle of the clip, you'll hear an MMPI member say, "flash." Just before that word, however, this unknown female voice says something else. To us it sounds like "Fred" or "Frank."

Upon further review of the MMPI audio, we found another possible EVP. This clip has been forwarded to MMPI for their further analysis. As of this writing we have not received their results.

The EVP captured appears to be a male voice. We believe it says, "Knife… hit… die in hell." The word *hell* was pronounced *hale*, almost with a southern drawl.

What immediately caught our attention in these audio clips were the words, "Fred" or "Frank" and "knife." Thinking back to the saloon's history, we remembered the knife fight between Frank Prena and Fred Kraemer. We wondered at the possibility of some residual energy replaying the event over and over again.

Unfortunately, during our investigation, we were not able to gather sufficient evidence to claim the saloon haunted. Of course, you just can't tell ghosts to come out and play if they don't want to. And we must admit the audio evidence collected by MMPI during their previous investigations is compelling.

The John A. Lau Saloon has a fascinating history that takes us back to Michigan's early lumbering days and a very colorful period in our state's history. We may never know all the violence or tragedies this saloon and town have seen.

The next time you're in Alpena, we suggest you stop by the John A. Lau Saloon. You may get lucky enough to catch a glimpse of Agnes, John, Fred, or Frank. Be sure to come with a big appetite so you can enjoy their really delicious *lumberjack food*,… and watch out for those pint-sized hockey players.

Story Seven
Cadieux Café

Detroit, Michigan
Web site: www.HauntedTravelsMI.com
Secret Room Password: c35d
Paranormal Investigative Team:
Organization for the Research and Science
of the Paranormal

This story deals not so much with a haunting, though the Cadieux Café is said to be haunted. Instead, the real story behind this investigation is of a much more *sensitive* nature… psychically speaking.

We first learned about the Cadieux Café from Ivan Tunney, group leader of the Organization for the Research and Science of the Paranormal (ORSP). The Cadieux is an old neighborhood watering hole in Detroit. It's been a fun place to hang out for decades.

We're not sure exactly how old the building is, but we understand it was one of Detroit's noted speakeasies during the prohibition days of the 1920s, known as "The Roaring Twenties." It was a time of prosperity, decadence, and extreme conservatism. It was also a turbulent period when alcohol was banned. Illegal speakeasies (bars) sprung up across the country and powerful underworld gangs were in charge.

During that decade, Michigan was controlled by the Mafia, Blackhand, and Purple Gang. Al Capone, of course, was the ringleader of the Chicago Mafia, which also controlled the west side of Michigan. The Purple Gang ran the Detroit area. Its ringleaders were the four Bernstein brothers (Abe, Joe, Raymond, and Izzy).

Rumor has it that the Cadieux had a long history with the Purples. The gang supplied the owner with bootlegged liquor. Ivan Tunney had done some advance research on events that may have transpired at the Cadieux.

One day the owner, a man who went by the name of Whitey, decided to start making his own liquor. The Purples found out. They came to "the joint," pulled out a shotgun loaded with lightweight birdshot, and fired, point blank. It didn't kill him, but it did scar his face for life. Whitey was left with a lasting reminder of what would happen should he try the same thing again.

Those early gangster days are over. Since then, the Cadieux has been a social hub for metro Detroit's Belgian population and the local neighborhood.

The Devos family has owned the restaurant and bar since the early 1960s, keeping the interior much like its early speakeasy days.

Even today, they continue the Belgium tradition and are known for their steamed mussels and feather bowling. They also feature over a dozen varieties of Belgium beer. To attract the younger crowds (21 to 35), they bring in live bands on weekends and Karaoke on Wednesday nights.

This evening, we were headed to the Cadieux Café to meet with Ivan Tunney, leader of ORSP, along with his wife Linda, and Lead Investigator Danise Lyon. Ivan also brought along a sensitive on this investigation, Dan Brunner.

Dan was given the address of the Cadieux just a couple of hours before he left home in the Battle Creek area. We felt confident he knew nothing of the owner or the bar's history prior to his arrival.

Ivan Tunney discusses his plans for the evening

We were introduced to Ron Devos, an owner of the Cadieux. Before interviewing Ron, Ivan sent Dan off to another room so he wouldn't overhear the conversation. At that point, Ron began to tell us about his family and the paranormal activity at the bar.

Dan Brunner, Danise Lyon, and Linda Tunney relaxing while they can

His parents bought the bar when Ron was just a little boy. They lived in the back room for the first few years. Ron clearly remembers those early days. His father, Robert, and mother, Yvonne, would take care of the bar while Grandfather Alfred baby-sat Ron and his sister.

Yvonne was "the heart and soul" of the establishment while Robert was "the brains." Growing

Ron Devos talks about the café

up, Ron remembers the long hours his parents worked. He fondly recalls mingling with the patrons. Life seemed pretty good back then.

October 1973, Grandfather Alfred passed away while sleeping in his bedroom behind the bar. Alfred was nearly ninety years old. He had a long and happy life. More tragedy would soon follow.

It was not long after Alfred's death that Ron's father, Robert, became ill. There were problems with his lungs. Robert's breathing became more labored. What the doctors diagnosed was completely unexpected.

For many years, Robert's hobby was pigeon racing, a popular sport in those days. He kept his coops on the bar's roof and cared for the pigeons religiously. What

Robert Devos loved pigeon racing

Robert had contracted was a condition called "pigeon handler's disease" or "pigeon lung." This is similar to Black Lung or Coalminer's Lung Disease. In this case, the lungs are filled with pigeon dust making it increasingly difficult to breathe. There was no cure. Robert eventually succumbed to the condition in February 1978.

Yvonne Devos was the "heart and soul" of the café

After Robert's death, Yvonne, Ron, and his sister, Fern, ran the Cadieux. Yvonne continued to play a major role in the bar's operation. It was a passion and huge part of her life. She was there practically every day attending to business and laughing with customers. Even after she was diagnosed with cancer, she continued to work until the time she became seriously ill. Yvonne passed away July 1993. To this day, there are those who still claim to see her spirit sitting at her favorite chair near the bar.

Ron and his employees have all experienced some kind of phenomenon, including moving objects and apparitions. He told us some of his own personal experiences.

A regular occurrence is the faucet turning on in the back bathroom. One night, while alone, Ron heard the water running. He went back and found it going full blast. The sink was filled to the brim. Starring in astonishment, he watched as the faucet turned off and the sink drained.

Another time, Ron and an employee were in the restaurant talking when they heard the pitcher behind the back ledge of the bar hit the floor. This was a surprise because the ledge the pitcher was on has a steep angle and lip making it nearly impossible for anything to fall off. Even more surprising, there was no one behind the bar when it happened. Other unusual experiences reported are glasses and bottles falling for no apparent reason.

One time, a painter, working late one evening, clearly heard footsteps going down to the basement. He followed the footsteps but found no one. Unusual incidents have also occurred in the feather bowling alley. Light bulbs have suddenly shattered when the lights were turned off and no one was in the area.

One of Ron's female employees had another experience. Laurie had come in early one morning to set things up at the bar. While getting things ready, she looked up and saw Ron's deceased mother, Yvonne, sitting at the corner of the bar. Ron called Laurie shortly after she saw the apparition. He was surprised for a moment when she answered the phone, "She sounded just like my mother. Even the same accent."

On another occasion, an employee was working in the bar and saw a woman in a flowered dress walk into the back room. There was no one there at the time.

Since the Cadieux was such a big part of her life, some believe Yvonne's spirit remains. The same is said about Ron's father. A male apparition has appeared in the basement. Some believe this may be Robert.

After Ron's interview, Ivan went to get Dan but stopped at a table near the bar. He leaned over, resting his hands on the glass top. Beneath his hands was an assortment of memorabilia spanning forty years that

Ivan drawn to the table

included old bottle caps, cigar wrappers, license plates, etc. Ivan was sensing something at the table that belonged to someone very close to the business. It had something to do with the bar's history… nothing dangerous or malevolent. He felt that whatever was in the table belonged to this person.

Ivan looked at Ron and said, "Did your dad smoke cigars?" Ron indicated that he had. Ivan pointed to the El Producto cigar box that was under the glass. Ron nodded, "El Producto."

"Is that your dad's?" Ivan asked.

"Yup."

"It belonged to your dad?"

"Yeah, probably. That's what he smoked, El Producto."

Ivan nodded his head in acknowledgement. His feelings had been confirmed. He then turned and opened the door to let Dan begin his walk-through of the building. Dan entered smiling. He had been locked up in the feather bowling area for nearly an hour.

"You have a jokester!" he said. As he explained, this friendly spirit likes to play pranks like throwing things in the alley, opening and closing doors, or tossing pitchers and glasses around.

Moving to the main bar, Dan paused for a moment and then wove through the kitchen without hesitation heading to the bathroom in the back. He opened the door and turned the left faucet handle on and off saying, "He likes to do this."

"Who?" I asked.

"The jokester."

"Who is this jokester?"

"Hmm, don't know."

Dan chose the very bathroom in which Ron had seen the faucet turn on and off. He then walked down the hallway and entered the backroom to the right. This room was now used for storage. Dan thought for a moment.

Dan prepares for his walk through

The jokester loves to play here

"There's a Bud or Albert." He paused briefly, "How about Alfred?"

"What do you feel about that person? Anything?" I asked.

Dan's response, "He's old."

"Like how old?"

"Really old," Dan smiled. "He goes by Bud... Alfred or Bud."

"Do you feel happiness or sadness here?

"No. He's content."

Dan felt Alfred died in the room. We stood silent saying nothing yet knowing that Dan was absolutely accurate. He was in Grandfather Alfred's room. This is where the old man passed away when he was nearly ninety years old.

Leaving the room, Dan sensed a woman's presence in the hallway. He mentioned that her energy might be visible to other people. I asked him why she stayed in the hallway. He responded, "I don't know. Maybe she lived down here too. It's almost like this is a home."

Again, Dan was correct. Ron's staff had reported seeing a female apparition in this area. This is also the section of the building where Ron's family had lived years before. Most would not realize that, however, since the rooms had long been converted to storage areas and offices.

With that, Dan moved out of the kitchen and headed directly to the basement. Here he immediately sensed "the pigeon man."

Dan's hand moved to his chest. "He makes me want to grab my chest. He's got a problem breathing"

He rubbed his hand across his temple, trying to make sense of the signals he was receiving. Shaking his head, it didn't make sense to him. "Did he swallow a pigeon?" Dan looked confused.

Shadows seen in the hallway

He continued, "This is your cigar smoker. But that's not what it is [that caused his chest to hurt]."

"Well," he said in frustration "I don't get it. I can feel my chest, and I'm seeing... pigeons... like a lot of them!" Then, with certainty, Dan looked at us. "That's what he died from."

At this point, Dan quickly continued. "This guy belongs here. He either lived upstairs or he owned the bar. This is... Bob."

We were absolutely amazed at Dan's ability to

Dan talks about Robert's breathing problems

An apparition is seen in this area

identify such a rare disease and death. It was equally surprising that he was able to identify Bob (Robert), Ron's father, as "the pigeon man."

Dan was unaware of his remarkable accuracy. He saw another male spirit in the main room of the bar. The man didn't die at the bar, but it was his last memory. The male presence appeared to be moving from the main entrance towards the bar.

Dan said, "He's trying to get to his barstool and never reaches it. He's trying so hard to get the barstool. He just wants to sit down and have a beer, and he can't make it. He can't make it."

Bartender tells his story

We later learned from Ron that some of his staff had seen the frequent, shadowy apparition of a figure walking through the doorway. It disappears before reaching the bar. He also mentioned that a long-time patron of the bar had been killed just outside the restaurant many years earlier. We wondered if his spirit might also remain at the Cadieux.

After that, Dan's role was complete. It was time for Ivan to begin setting up audio and video equipment using Dan's recommendations and Ivan's own feelings. Motion detectors and a video camera were placed by the front entrance, where the apparition was seen. Another camera was facing the bar. Audio recorders were placed in the bar, bowling alley, basement, and back rooms.

Linda and Danise began setting up equipment. I had often wondered why the hours between midnight and 3:00 A.M. were considered the most active times. Ivan shared the common theory.

The team sets up equipment

Ivan explains the significance of the dead hour

"Some people believe that the force that keeps us apart from the next realm is thinnest around midnight because of the changing of the day. But the other school of thought and the one I subscribe to is 3:00 A.M. This hour is known at the *anti-hour* or the *dead hour* but that is actually the opposite time that Christ died on the cross. Sometimes if you have something particularly malignant, it will appear at 3:00 A.M. It doesn't mean that it is malignant because it appears at 3:00 A.M., that's just been my experience with it. It seems to be a commonly accepted theory."

With that, he went off to set up trigger objects. Baby powder was sprinkled around drink glasses, and beer bottles were placed on a few tables. The powder would help identify the movement of objects. Once that was complete our vigil began.

The group gathered in the main bar and silently waited. An occasional question was asked in the hope of eliciting any spirit response. At times, people would travel to other parts of the building to monitor equipment and check for unusual sounds or movements. As the evening progressed without obvious activity, Ivan attempted to provoke the spirits.

Ivan's voice became belligerent, and he began to curse in order to elicit a response. Finally, he said, "If you don't like me talkin' like this, all you have to do is tell me and I'll stop. It's your place!" Ivan went on like this for several minutes. Nothing happened.

In the early hours of the morning, Ivan called the investigation to an end. The audio and video we collected would be carefully reviewed over the upcoming days.

Ivan taunts the spirits to show themselves

Unfortunately, after careful examination of all recorded materials, nothing was detected.

If the Cadieux does have active spirits, they chose not to show themselves during this investigation. Photographs and video clips of the investigation, including segments of Ron's interview and Dan's remarkable revelations, can be found in our Web site's Secret Room.

Though there is no evidence to support a haunting at the Cadieux, what we witnessed was a truly remarkable display of sensitive power. Virtually everything Dan mentioned was validated by Ron.

Now, it is true that, with a little bit of effort, the Cadieux Café story and Robert's tragic death can be found on the Internet. It is sometimes difficult to determine if a psychic or sensitive has real intuitive power or just good Internet research skills. We dismiss that possibility for this investigation.

Extreme care was given not to reveal the destination to Dan until just before he left his Battle Creek home. Adding to that, there was no way Dan could have known about Grandfather Alfred's name or death, the exact location of his death, or several other facts that he correctly identified. We were all quite amazed at Dan's accuracy that evening.

Ivan and the ORSP team used a very professional approach throughout the investigation. If evidence is captured on a future visit, it will be placed in our Web site's Secret Room.

Haunted or not, the Cadieux Café's steamed mussels, feather bowling, and Belgium beers make this one heck of a great place to come. Definitely check it out… and, who knows, maybe the ghosts will come out for you.

Story Eight
South Lyon Hotel

South Lyon, Michigan
Web site: www.HauntedTravelsMI.com
Secret Room Password: sa2rd
Paranormal Investigative Team:
Shadow Land Investigators

It was a cold, bleak January afternoon. We stared out the window watching the snow fall. We were having trouble finding the right words to open the new chapter in our Haunted Travels book. Thank goodness the phone rang because we were going nowhere. It was Charla calling from Shadow Land Investigators, a paranormal group based in Ann Arbor. She was inviting us to a hunt at the South Lyons Hotel. Charla mentioned they had investigated the hotel for some time with some interesting experiences. She thought it might make a good addition to our book. We agreed.

Despite the name, the South Lyon Hotel is really a restaurant and pub catering to the local community. Located in southwestern Oakland County, it is a fun, casual restaurant with plenty of comfort foods. Their menu ranges from pizza and burgers to Teriyaki Bourbon Salmon and Mike's Meatloaf. The relaxed interior merges the 1900s with the twenty-first century. Tandem bicycles, antiques, and sports memorabilia decorate the walls.

We met Charla White, Robb Kaczor, and Joan St. John from Shadow Land at the restaurant on a blustery January night with temperatures hovering near the zero mark. Warming up over coffee, Corry Bala, one of the restaurant's owners joined us. Together they briefed us on the building's paranormal activity and history.

Corry described the strange occurrences that are frequently experienced by him and his staff. These activities include shadows, full body apparitions, and voices. There appears to be a re-occurring problem with TVs turning on and even automatic towel dispensers operating in the ladies rooms

Corry Bala, Co-owner

with no one nearby. Charla and Robb concurred. They had seen a shadow ascending the stairs on a previous investigation. Corry mentioned one of the women working for him had several terrifying experiences with an apparition in the ladies room. We were looking forward to interviewing her at another time.

Eric Blotkamp, a restaurant manager, recounted his personal experiences. One day, while in the Oak Room,

Eric Blotkamp, Manager

Eric heard a voice behind him. The voice was definitely male and said, "Help me." He turned in surprise and found no one there. The voice was so clear. He was shocked to find no one around. This phrase has been heard by other employees on the second floor. Our interviews with Corry and Eric can be seen in our Web site's Secret Room.

Knowing the history of a location can be very important in understanding the paranormal activity. We were fortunate that Charla had done a lot of the initial research on the town and restaurant. Its history takes us back to 1832. The village of South Lyon was a little cow town with not much there except the widow Thompson's log cabin and country store. Once the railroad lines were built, the little community began to grow, adding stores, post office, and cemetery.

By 1867, to accommodate the railroad passengers, Baker Hopkins decided to build a hotel. The problem was the location. He wanted to build it on the cemetery. To accommodate Hopkins, all the bodies were moved to a new cemetery, and the hotel was built.

South Lyon Hotel, early days

Of course, everyone thought all the bodies were removed… but were they? It's very possible some remains were left undiscovered. There is a strong possibility that some of the deceased were never moved to the new cemetery. They may still remain under the foundation of the hotel.

For the next hundred years, the community and hotel went through numerous changes. Perhaps one of the more colorful times in the hotel's history is the 1970s. The hotel became a popular hangout for biker gangs and was known for wild parties and bar fights. It had become a dangerous place, and city residents stayed away. The poor and transients with little money occupied the second floor apartments.

On July 18, 1977, a fire ravaged the hotel. An article taken from the *South Lyon Newspaper* later that year recounts the event. It started when someone probably threw a cigarette butt into a waste basket on the first floor. Omer Talmedge Duncan, a down-and-out resident of the hotel, was nearby when he saw the smoke and rushed back. The hotel was consumed with flames when he got to the front doors. Omer entered to retrieve his few belongings. The blaze raced up the stairs to the apartments. The article stated that Omer tried to leave down the stairway and was overcome with heat and smoke. They later found his remains in the ruins of the hotel.

After the fire, the building was repaired. It remained a bar and restaurant with upstairs apartments throughout most of the 1980s until new owners took over. Paul Baker and his family bought the building in 1988. In the early 1990s, the upstairs apartments were removed, and the second floor was changed into a bakery. Later, the bakery was converted to an expanded dining area and bar.

Paul Baker brought Corry Bala in as a co-partner. Paul and Corry weren't just working partners; they were also good friends. Corry considered Paul a mentor. Their restaurant business was booming when something happened. Paul suffered a sudden and unexpected heart attack that proved fatal. To this day, Corry fondly talks about his former partner's energy and enthusiasm. Paul was involved with four restaurants, but it was the South Lyon Hotel that he loved the most.

It is thought that Paul and Omer are some of the spirits remaining at this restaurant. That's what we were hoping to discover on this investigation.

For some time, Shadow Land has been investigating suspect activity at the South Lyon Hotel. They believe the place to have a high degree of activity, including demonic. We were eager to join them for a night to see what would transpire.

The Shadow Land's team relies heavily on their sensitivity and intuitive nature for investigations.

Paul Baker,
former owner, deceased

Courtesy of the South Lyon Hotel

Joan is the lead psychic. Her abilities are widely known. Joan has helped families, local police departments, and the FBI in their search for missing people and criminal investigations.

Charla and Robb don't claim to have the same skills as Joan but do believe they have some level of sensitivity. In fact, Robb does not interview people prior to equipment setup but relies on his feelings to determine active locations.

Robb Kaczor and Charla White
set up equipment

The team began to place equipment based on their senses and phenomena they had witnessed during previous investigations at the South Lyon Hotel. These paranormal activities included shadows and apparitions on stairways and hallways. They had also experienced unusual energy spikes and noises in the kitchen. Though not recorded, the team believes objects have moved in the second floor Oak Room (a room used for private events). Once everything was positioned, Joan began her work.

During Joan's previous visits, the hotel's basement seemed to be a trigger for her senses, and she wanted to start there. Her earlier visits had detected a demonic family trapped below. She was interested to see if they would reveal themselves again.

Kat and I have been on well over two dozen investigations and had never encountered demonic spirits. It would be interesting to see what would happen.

We left the warm comfort of the restaurant single-file to face the harsh wind and blowing snow that followed us to the icy outside entrance of the basement. Leaving the chill, we descended into the bleakness of another time. Dirt floors and stone walls marked the history of this building. Bare, vacuous light bulbs hung from the ceilings casting deep shadows along passageways. In spots, we ducked our heads to avoid low beams and the eerie tendrils of spider webs. Scuffing up the dust as we walked, Kat and I became very aware that the dirt beneath our feet had once been a cemetery. Some of the bodies may still remain.

The group halted in the back room. Silent for a moment, our eyes adjusted to the gloomy interior. One of the things first noticed was a hole in the ceiling that had been patched up. Corry told us it was the original stairway to the hotel. After the fire, the first stairway was blocked off and a new entrance built during renovation.

The old stairway was positioned directly below the Oak Room and Ladies Room. Omer Talmedge Duncan died on the stairs during the 1977 fire. It began to make sense that the Oak Room and Ladies Room were sites of paranormal activity. Omer's horrific death was likely to have occurred in or near these rooms. Omer's energy could remain trapped on these stairs pleading for help. This could be the reason for Eric hearing a male voice call for help in the Oak Room and for other reported paranormal activity in these locations.

We next focused our eyes on a cross resting on a mound of dirt by the wall. On closer inspection, however, the cross turned out to be just a broken table leg. The Shadow Land group told us not to dismiss it so easily. It was not the table leg but the symbol of a cross that was important. The cross was not to be disturbed or removed. The act of moving it would release the demonic family held captive by this religious symbol. Though Kat and I had our doubts, Shadow Land and several other groups who had visited truly believe this to be the case. We respected their opinions and concerns for caution.

Within moments, the demon family began to materialize for Joan. She saw the father, mother, and young boy against the farthest wall. From the room on the right, Joan noticed a young girl peeking out with lizard-like characteristics. Kat and I looked at each other. Nothing was visible to us. We had to rely on Joan's unique skills.

Joan began, "They can't breathe... they can't breathe. I feel someone was strangled."

Pointing to the back wall, behind the mound of dirt, she continued. "Three of them are standing there. They're just standing there. Their clothes are torn. They say they can't pass... they can't pass [the cross]. Margaret... is warning us. She doesn't like it down here."

This symbol cannot be moved according to Joan

She saw a female and male adult and an eight- or ten-year-old boy. "There's a girl. She's peeking around the wall... she's more lizard shaped."

"They want to own this place. They say... this is our place."

Kat asked, "Why are you here?"

Joan responded for them, "We own this place. This is our place... we were put here. We're not leaving."

Kat asked, "How were you put here?"

Joan sighed, as if in distress. "There's such a pain in my heart. This one... it's as if her heart was cut out."

Joan continued, "It was like a ritualistic kind of thing... she's showing me the heart was removed. She told me... we were treated like vampires... we were hunted, we were hunted."

"They were black magic practitioners, so people feared them."

Kat asked, "What year is it?

Joan's reply, "1783."

Joan spoke more about the presence of the little girl in this area. She described her as a lizard-shaped, inhuman form appearing much like a griffin. Charla asked the next question.

"If we were to remove the cross, what would you do?"

"We would go for your throat!"

Kat asked, "Do you have a name, what is it?"

"The man says his name is John... the woman is Emily. It's almost as if they pretended to be Christians. They fit in well. Benjamin is the boy. Christina is the girl, but they call her Trina. They fed off the fears of others."

Joan talks to the spirits

Charla asked, "Why did you start the fire in the hotel?"

"We needed him." Joan said, speaking for them.

"Did you get him?"

"Of course."

Corry and Eric ask Joan questions about the spirit

Charla asked, "Where is he now?"

"He's being held down by the legs. He can't move."

"What was his name?" Kat asked

"He's down here too. The howling is him... the howling voice. He did no harm to anyone but they kept him here to feed off of his energy. That's how they survive, by feeding off his energy."

This time Corry sent out a question. "What is his name?"

"Ed."

Joan continued to tell us that the family was accused of demon worship by the townspeople and was tracked down and killed. Their hearts were cut out. We remained for some time, asking questions and attempting to provoke the family with no noticeable response.

After some time, everyone decided to return to the warm interior of the restaurant. The Shadow Land group handles investigations by placing equipment at key locations. Once set up, they remain focused on watching the monitors for possible activity with periodic equipment checks. During this investigation, they did not conduct actual EVP sessions. Throughout the night and early morning, everyone remained attentive to the monitor screens and the sounds of the restaurant.

Corry sits in the spot where Joan senses a demon family

On previous investigations, the group had seen a shadow figure appear moving up the staircase from the first floor bar. This phenomenon occurred between 2:30 A.M. and 3:30 A.M., which could mark a possible residual haunting. For that reason, they focused one of their video cameras on the stairway this evening.

About 2:30 A.M. Kat and I left the group and went up to the second floor Oak Room, just in case the shadow might make an appearance there. After approximately twenty minutes, Robb entered the room. He looked serious.

"You might want to come downstairs."

"Yeah?" Kat asked, "Is something going on?"

"We just caught the shadow going around the corner over here on the video."

"Was it coming upstairs?"

Robb nodded, "Coming up. A little black shadow coming up."

We immediately checked the second floor. Nothing was seen or heard. Heading back downstairs we met Charla and Joan at the monitors.

Kat met up with the ladies, "So, you got a shadow?"

"Yeah, it went right by me." Joan responded.

Charla added, "One was going up the steps."

"Was that what you remember seeing before?"

Robb said, "No. This was entirely different. This was a shadow the other thing was a lot more solid."

"Could you see if it was in human form?"

"No. It was just black. It had no form."

No noises or temperature changes were felt before, during, or after the event. The remainder of the night was very quiet. No further activity was detected.

Unfortunately, after final

Stairs where Charla and Robb
saw the shadow

review, the shadow seen by the group was not captured on video. On a previous investigation, they did record an EVP taken in the Oak Room. It is a single word, "What." We have included this in our Secret Room.

A bit unsettling, Kat captured a bizarre noise that sounded somewhere between a raspy breath and an eerie laugh. This EVP was recorded on her video camera in the basement at about 12:30 A.M. It can be heard in our Secret Room.

Shadow Land will continue their investigation of the South Lyon Hotel. Should they provide us with further evidence, we will include it in our Web site's Secret Room. As of this writing, however, we do not have sufficient evidence to validate an actual haunting at the restaurant.

We certainly enjoyed our time with Shadow Land. They are a down-to-earth, welcoming group that provided a different approach to paranormal investigation. It was also a pleasure to meet Corry and some of the very friendly South Lyon staff.

Disembodied voices have been heard in the Oak Room

The story of the haunting does not end here. A few weeks after the investigation, we had the opportunity of interviewing the young housekeeper, Shigella, who had witnessed the apparition of a man in the ladies room. Shigella's sincerity in recounting her story was so convincing we had to include it.

The events that happened to Shigella occurred over the span of a few years. The first occurred when she was cleaning the ladies room on the second floor. She felt a sudden sadness and a "bad feeling." Turning toward the towel dispenser, Shigella saw a hovering shadow. The motion-activated dispenser suddenly began rolling out paper. Frightened, she left and immediately called her husband. She refused to come back to work for several months.

The young woman eventually returned to the South Lyon but would only venture into the upstairs bathroom if someone were with her. One morning, around 9:00 A.M., she broke the promise made to herself and ventured into the bathroom to restock paper. In those few seconds the sudden feeling of sadness returned. Shigella turned to leave and abruptly stopped. A man blocked her exit. Unable to speak, frozen in place, she stared at him for about a minute.

His image was solid, and she clearly recalled every detail. He was of medium height with brown eyes and longish, straight brown hair parted in the middle. His cheeks were sunken and pale. The man wore a long-sleeved white shirt with dark brown trousers and suspenders. Shigella did not see his feet. Silently, he stood staring at her. His shrunken lips parted into a lifeless smile showing stained, decayed teeth.

She didn't return to work for five months. All went well for a while until her most recent and final encounter. It happened just a few days before our interview. Around noon, Shigella went to the second floor ladies room using a trash can to prop open the door. It closed behind her. Thinking it had slipped, she went back to reposition it. He was there again. The same male figure she had seen before.

"Oh my God!" she cried and turned to run, hesitating briefly to move the trash can aside. At that moment the man took hold of the end of her shirt as if to stop her.

He spoke one word, "Well," then let her go.

For some time she was in shock and remained speechless. It wasn't until she arrived back home that Shigella noticed her upper arm was hurting, like it had been scratched.

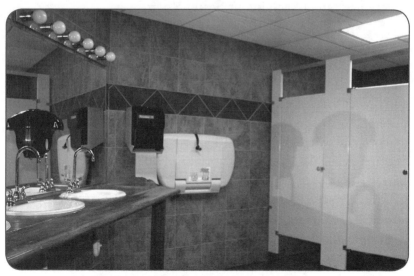

The location of Shigella's ghostly encounters

Going to a mirror, she pulled up her shirtsleeve and looked in stunned surprise. She called her husband to see. He gasped, "Oh my God, it's a hand!"

With that statement, Shigella removed her coat and pulled up the sleeve of her blouse and showed Kat her arm. There it was, four days later, the distinct bruising marks of four fingers.

Of course, we have no idea how those marks got there. One thing is certain, Shigella was absolutely

The marks left by the male spirit

sincere in what she told us. The fear was obvious in the woman's eyes when we asked her to return to the bathroom and in her retelling of the story. A color photo and video interview of her experience can be seen in our Secret Room.

Corry, Charla, and Robb believe Shigella may have seen the ghost of Omer Talmedge Duncan, the man who died in the hotel fire in 1977. Some believe that while coming down the main stairway a timber fell across Omer's lower legs, pinning him down and preventing his escape. Perhaps that is why Shigella did not see his feet. As of this writing, we have not found a picture of Omer to compare with the description Shigella gave us. Should one become available after publication, we will post it in this story's Secret Room.

Shigella's intriguing experience and Shadow Land Investigators strong belief that the South Lyon Hotel is haunted make this a compelling story. Continued investigations may give us the evidence needed to support a claim of paranormal activity.

Story Nine
Bowers Harbor Inn
Restaurant

Old Mission Peninsula, Michigan
Web site: www.HauntedTravelsMI.com
Secret Room Password: ka46t
Paranormal team:
West Michigan Ghost Hunters Society

The Grand Traverse region of Michigan has long-been one of the state's most popular tourist destinations. With unique shops, wineries, golf courses, and the beautiful blue waters of Lake Michigan, it's hard to imagine that behind the happy smiles of residents and vacationers there are tragedies from the past that linger.

This visit to the area would lead us to one of those tragic stories and a beautiful restaurant on Old Mission Peninsula called Bowers Harbor Inn. Known for its well-prepared cuisine and scenic/remote location, it has been serving guests for decades.

Set back from Peninsula Drive and nearly hidden by majestic oaks and pines overlooking West Grand Traverse Bay, a winding driveway takes you to the inn's entrance. The inn is reminiscent of turn-of-the-century opulence. Particular attention in its construction is revealed in rich woods, imported tiles, marble fireplaces, and intricate designs that will unveil new detail with each return visit.

Of course, as beautiful as this home is, the food remains the primary reason people return. Its menu features creatively prepared cuisine. Presentation and service are exceptional, and your waitperson will always have a story about his or her encounter with "Genevieve's ghost." More on that later.

Casually elegant dining

The informal Bowery

For those seeking some comfort food at modest prices, the Bowery is a fun, casual place. It is the oldest part of the inn and the last remaining section of the original farmhouse that first stood on the land before the Stickneys purchased it. This area later became the canning room of Genevieve Stickney, said to be the spirit that haunts the restaurant.

The "Genevieve Legend" handed down through the decades is a tale of jealousy, infidelity, and suicide. As the story goes, Genevieve was an obese, jealous woman. When she grew older, she suffered from infirmity. Charles, her husband, installed an elevator to transport Genevieve between floors. He also hired a nurse to help care for her.

The story continues that Charles took the nurse as his mistress. Genevieve detested the woman, fearing her husband would leave his wealth to the mistress. Upon Charles' demise, Genevieve's greatest fears came true. Charles Stickney bequeathed all his riches to the nurse leaving Genevieve with only the Bowers Harbor home. Distraught and deeply depressed, Genevieve hung herself in the elevator. To this day it is said her restless spirit haunts Bowers Harbor Inn.

An interesting story, of course, but is the legend true? Did Charles have an affair and leave all his wealth to his mistress? Is it possible he would disinherit his wife after more than fifty years of marriage? Did Genevieve really hang herself in the elevator? Perhaps most importantly, does her ghostly spirit remain at Bowers?

We spoke with several employees of the restaurant who claimed to have encountered paranormal activity. We also watched an interesting video produced by George Meredith called, "Dinner and a Ghost." George's video captured some

Did Genevieve hang herself in the elevator?

interesting phenomena that included unexplainable dancing lights along with visible movement on the grand stairway. It made us very curious. What was really going on at Bowers Harbor Inn?

We contacted Nicole Bray, founder of West Michigan Ghost Hunters Society (WMGHS) for the investigation. She was happy to help. We agreed on a time and date. Her co-partner and EVP specialist, Rob, along with her technical specialist, Brad, and core investigator, Bob, would join us on the hunt.

A few weeks later we met Nicole's team along with Tim Kleynenberg, co-owner of Bowers. Tim took us on a brief tour of the restaurant pointing out the most active areas: (1) The women's bathroom on the second floor. Guests have claimed to hear disembodied voices. Faucets turn on and toilets flush by themselves. (2) The staircase leading to the upstairs bathrooms has reported mists, unusual flashing lights, and visions of a woman. (3) The elevator where Genevieve was said to have hung herself supposedly has cold spots and "feelings of dread." The elevator is no longer operable, but when it was, there were reports of it mysteriously moving between floors. (4) The main dining area has reports of place settings being moved and candles levitating. (5) Some claim to have seen Genevieve's image in her gold gilded mirror, located in the foyer. (6) Genevieve's photograph and wall hangings have a habit of falling off the wall. (7) Unusual mists have been seen outdoors. (8) The Bowery, which is the oldest part of the home and an original portion of the old farmhouse, has reported at least one saltshaker being lifted over the ledge of the second floor railing and falling to the floor below. There were also reports of strange lights emanating from the bar area.

Genevieve's reflection has been seen in this mirror

We thanked Tim for the tour as Nicole's group began setting up their base station in the Bowery

Pictures have mysteriously fallen off the wall

restaurant. In that section, they also wired an infrared video camera targeting the bar. In the meantime, Bev went outside to take exterior photographs of the property as I headed over to the second floor conference room to assemble my video gear. This is the room that was said to have been Genevieve's bedroom. We were told Charles had a separate room. Later, we would find that both Charles and Genevieve shared this room.

Kat Tedsen, Nicole Bray, and Tim Kleynenberg

The room was spacious and truly remarkable with deep and rich woods. A beautiful stained glass window highlighted a quiet sitting alcove and, to the side, a small fireplace framed with Austrian tiles. Perhaps most remarkable was the painting of Genevieve that hung above the fireplace. It was an

Genevieve's Portrait in the conference room

intricately detailed portrait of Genevieve as an innocent, vulnerable young woman far removed from the jealous, obese woman legend describes. The portrait was mesmerizing and, somehow, seemed so lonely in this room now lined with tables.

Removed from the downstairs chatter of guests, it was remarkably quiet. As I turned to open the camera bag, something caught the corner of my eye. Looking up, I was surprised to see a series of lights flicker across Genevieve's portrait. Three, maybe four, times they flashed and then were gone.

The illumination consisted of two vertical columns each with three or four diamond-shaped lights. I immediately looked out the windows to see if there were any outside lights that would have caused this unusual reflection. There were no cars coming up or leaving the driveway, and the exterior ground lights were not on. Thinking it was my imagination, I continued with my camera assembly when, again, the diamond flashes flickered across the portrait. This time I knew it wasn't my imagination. What the heck?

I attempted to recreate the light using my flashlight to reflect off surfaces. Nothing came close to what I had seen. I quickly finished assembly of my video gear and was ready. I aimed the camera on the portrait and waited. Minutes passed… nothing. Darn it!

When Nicole entered the room, I mentioned the event. She nodded and set one of their video cameras to cover that section of the room for the duration of the evening. Unfortunately, the phenomena did not occur again. Frustrating, but that's the way things frequently go.

Meanwhile, Bev was outside getting exterior photos. She was eager to get the grounds covered before dark to avoid using a flash. As she began taking photos of the trees, a mist suddenly appeared from seemingly nowhere. She clicked off a couple of shots. The

Photos capture outdoor mist

mist appeared to move downward. In an instant, it disappeared in the camera's lens. She pulled the camera down to see where the mist had gone. To her total surprise, it had formed around her legs. As she positioned the camera to get another photo, the mist disappeared. It was that quick.

Coming back inside, Bev shared her experience with me. I asked if she had felt or sensed anything unusual while that was going on. She shook her head no. She hadn't even felt a cool humidity that might be expected with a mist.

It was just about then the restaurant's chef, Colin, approached us. Colin came across some interesting discoveries in the building and wanted to share them with us. We followed him as he revealed places that few employees ever used — or wanted to use.

There were unknown, walled-off tunnels that burrowed under the foundation of

Chef Colin showed us some secret places

the inn. A small, tightly sealed screen was the only opening that revealed its dark interior. The beam from a small flashlight probed into the darkness revealing a variety of bottles, newspapers, and discarded clothing clearly from another era. It had obviously been used at some point in the home's history.

Colin's favorite little secret was outside. Taking us to the back of the inn, he bent under a staircase pulling overgrown shrubbery aside to reveal his prized discovery. Embedded in the foundation of the inn was a heart-shaped stone, its color a faded black. Obviously a symbol of love, it now seemed so forlorn hidden away from view. Our staring at it somehow seemed like an intrusion on its intimate message. We wondered if it had been placed there by the original owners of the home or by Charles during the rebuilding process.

At that point Chef Colin left, wishing us well with the investigation, and we went upstairs where Nicole and the group had gathered. All equipment was set and ready to go. Nicole gave our evening assignments, and the home went dark. The warm charm of the restaurant quickly faded into eerie shadows as we waited and listened.

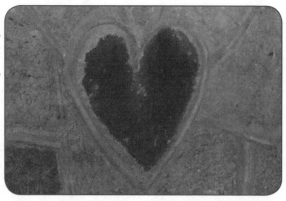

Who embedded the heart in the home's foundation?

Our first assignment was the ladies room, which is said to be Genevieve's former

The ladies' bathroom has reports of ghostly activity

sitting room. This area is considered one of the inn's most active locations with guests and staff reporting incidents of swinging lamps, disembodied voices, faucets turning on, and toilets flushing by themselves.

The first thing we did was check the bathroom faucets. We immediately noted the hot and cold handles were loose when turning them to the off position. A quick turn of the handle would stop the water, but a hard turn was required to completely shut them off. Having spoken to plumbers in the past, we knew that compression faucets, like these, could appear to turn on by themselves if the faucet stop is bad. Water pressure will build up in the pipes until the faucets are forced open.

The plumbers we spoke to also explained a completely natural cause of toilets appearing to flush on their own. It is commonly caused by a slow leak around the seal of the flapper, which drains the tank. In order to maintain the water level in the tank, the toilet turns itself on. We felt these explanations were likely the cause here.

With that resolved, we sat down to begin our EVP session. Our night-shot video camera and audio recorder captured every moment. During the hour, we saw or felt nothing unusual. Perhaps our recorded audio/video would later reveal what our senses could not.

Throughout the evening and into the early morning hours, our teams continued to regroup and relocate. We were particularly eager when it was our turn to monitor the entrance foyer, Harbor Room dining area, and staircase. It was on this stairway in the "Dinner and a Ghost" video that Meredith Productions captured several very unusual light anomalies and a startling movement along the stairway.

With our trusty still camera, night vision video camera, and audio recorders in hand, we silently waited. As would be the case throughout the evening, each session produced what we thought would be disappointing results. A little after 3:00 A.M. Nicole gathered us around for a brief wrap-up meeting. Except for my earlier incident with the flashing lights and Bev's experience with the mist, none of the group reported any personal experiences. Of course, hours of video and audio along with hundreds of still images needed to be closely reviewed before any conclusions could be made.

While WMGHS began to gather up their equipment, I walked from the Bowery dining area to the main restaurant, passing the hallway elevator. Something strangely familiar caused me to stop. What was it?

My eyes were drawn to the reflection of the hallway light cascading through the crossed lattice work of the elevator doors. The reflection cast vertical rows of diamond-shaped lights onto the elevator's back wall. I realized where I'd seen those lights. They were the same, *exactly the same*, as I had seen pass over Genevieve's portrait in the conference room earlier that evening.

The significance of this was stunning. I shared the experience with Bev and Nicole. They weren't too impressed and went off to continue collecting equipment. That is the part of a personal experience that makes it so frustrating. Only the person experiencing the event can appreciate its impact. That certainly was the case in this instance. I alone had

Diamond shaped lights matched those on the portrait

experienced the eerie portrait lights and the uncanny similarity of the elevator's reflection. It was as if I was sharing a personal, very private moment with Charles and Genevieve.

I stepped into the elevator and closed the door. The lattice reflections fell across my face just like the diamond lights had over Genevieve's portrait. A sudden sadness swept over me... an overwhelming sense of hopelessness. I can't explain what had caused it or why. Looking out into the hallway through the diamond shaped lights, I felt a growing sense that Genevieve had drawn me here and the answer to the true legend was, in fact, connected to this elevator.

It isn't certain how long I stood in the elevator, but the sound of Bev calling my name brought me back from whatever journey I had traveled. She saw me standing inside the small cubical.

"What the heck are you doing in there, and why haven't you been answering my calls?" A bit exasperated she said, "Come on, we're ready to leave." Bev approached the elevator, pushed back the lattice door and muttered, "I think I've found the reason for the cold spots by this elevator."

She ran her hand along the frame of the elevator and felt a cold draft coming from the elevator shaft. She smiled and said, "Solved!" My enthusiasm was somewhat diminished as I remained focused on my experience in the elevator. Was it just an overactive imagination or was a spirit trying to reach out?

Perhaps it was answered leaving the restaurant that morning. As we loaded our equipment in the car, I turned with my video camera one last time to scan the dark exterior. Suddenly, a light turned on in a second floor room. The curtains allowed only a sliver of light to escape. In an instant it was gone, as if someone or something was signaling to us one last time.

The following week, Nicole and her group found themselves immersed in tons of material that had to be painstakingly reviewed. Even Bev and I had hours of audio and video to go over. Where to begin? The review process was tedious and exhausting. No matter how bored, however, it's important to stay sharp and focused. Evidence can be overlooked in the blink of an eye.

Now, on to what we consider real evidence… and we did have some. The mysterious moving mist in Bev's exterior photographs was very curious. Of course, by the water, mist may occur on occasion. Because the mist traveled directly to Bev, however, this was an unusual event. The full color version is in our Web site's Secret Room.

Our quiet EVP session in the ladies room did hold some surprises. There appeared to be some valid audio evidence. Analyzing the audio was very difficult because the voices were very low and it was hard to enhance the sound. The EVPs sounded distinctly male, each with a raspy timber. When listening to the EVP evidence at our Web site, you will need to increase your volume to hear these low-decibel recordings.

In the first audio clip, I asked, "What year did you die? Do you know?" We believe the response was, "I need to know." In the second, I was asking if the Legend of Genevieve was just a story for publicity purposes. The response was, "So far."

Others have suggested the words are "no farm." If so, the ghostly voice did not answer my question. It may be responding to the fact that the Bowers farm is no more.

With the hours of video and audio we reviewed, Nicole and the WMGHS team had ten times more. Nicole's early report was disappointing. Their first run-through revealed nothing. The slow, tedious second review, however, came with the pay off.

Nicole e-mailed us a video clip with an understated note saying, "I think we have one piece of video evidence." Not expecting much, Bev and I downloaded the file. What we saw made us sit back in amazement. We played it again and again.

A stationary video camera on the second floor of the Bowery restaurant had been aimed toward the downstairs bar. At about 12:31 A.M. it captured some unusual movements.

First, a brief, rapid streak of light shot across the screen. Then slowly… ever so slowly, a second light evolved. Barely noticeable at first, emerging from behind the bar, it slowly took shape. Suspended in air, it gently moved across the room, appearing to pause momentarily before vanishing beyond the camera's lens.

At its closest point to the camera, this light anomaly resembled an oblong donut shape with a barely visible clear center. Some members of WMGHS said it reminded them of a saltshaker.

An unusual object floats across the Bowery

There had, of course, been the report of a saltshaker dropping from the second to the first floor at the Bowery. Whatever it was, there was no question that this anomaly was eerily unexplainable. View all the evidence at our Web site's Secret Room.

If this was some type of spirit energy, why did it choose this area of the restaurant to reside? The Bowery, Tim had mentioned, was the oldest part of the building. It is, as we found out, the last remaining part of the land's original farmhouse.

Genevieve used to can her fruits and make jellies and brandy in this area. Though she enjoyed these activities, it was more busy work while Charles was away. Why, then, would her spirit, if that's what this light represented, remain here?

Research was needed. Research that would ultimately reveal the truth behind the Genevieve Legend and the possible cause of the Bowers Harbor haunting.

We spent days in the Traverse City library and weeks searching online genealogy and blog sites. We even communicated with descendants of the family and were finally fortunate to find a dedicated Grand Traverse historian, Julie Schopieray. Julie was happy to help us out. Over the years, Julie had dedicated a good part of her time researching the history of the Stickneys and Bowers Harbor Inn. Between her research and ours, we began to put some of the pieces together.

Genevieve Worthen was born around 1863 to a well-to-do Lebanon, New Hampshire family. She was raised in this picturesque little town surrounded by rolling hills along a scenic river.

Courtesy of Bowers Harbor Inn

A young Genevieve Stickney

Slender and petite, Genevieve stood well under five feet. She was quiet and reserved with a bit of a stubborn streak. At the age of twenty-six, still unmarried, Genevieve met a dashing and gentle man, Charles Stickney. Charles, himself a man of short stature, was immediately taken with Genevieve, and they were soon married.

Charles was part owner of a shoe manufacturing company in Chicago. Shortly after the wedding, the happy couple moved to Chicago though Genevieve hated to leave Lebanon.

Charles Stickney

Courtesy of Bowers Harbor Inn

One day in 1909, Charles took a trip to the Traverse City area and Genevieve joined him. It was then the couple discovered an old, abandoned farmhouse and orchard on Old Mission Peninsula overlooking Grand Traverse Bay. Genevieve immediately fell in love with the scenic beauty of the location, which was very reminiscent of her Lebanon home.

At the time, Charles had most of his money invested in the family business and didn't have extra cash to buy the place, so Genevieve purchased the land (her name is on the original land deed). After some minor renovations, the old farmhouse became their summer home. Genevieve, who claimed to be part American Indian, gave the home an Indian name. She called it the *We-Gwa-Se-Min* Ranch, meaning beautiful cherry orchard.

Both Genevieve and Charles loved their place on Peninsula Drive. In fact, it was their only true home. According to census records and communication with family descendants, Charles and Genevieve owned no other home but Bowers. During late fall through early spring, they resided at hotels in Chicago and Grand Rapids.

It was in the 1920s that the fire struck. A massive blaze, it consumed a good part of the old house. Had the neighbors not rallied to extinguish the flames, the fire would surely have taken out the farmland and surrounding homes. When the flames finally subsided, a good part of the home was gone. Genevieve was devastated. Charles consoled her and promised that they would build a bigger, even more beautiful home.

Together they worked with Genevieve's cousin, Kenneth Worthen, to design a new home. Kenneth was a noted architect, and no expense was spared in the restoration. Only the finest woods were used. Austrian marble was brought in for the fireplaces, and stained glass features were added to enhance the elegance. What resulted is the beautiful home that is now Bowers Harbor Inn. The portion of the restaurant known as the Bowery is what remains of the original farmhouse.

As the years passed, Genevieve and Charles shared many great adventures together including exotic trips to the Far East and Europe. Eventually, the years took their toll and Genevieve became ill.

It got to a point where just walking was exhausting. Their good friend and family physician, Dr. Whinery, identified the problem. Genevieve's heart was failing. Charles, who had his own health problems, installed an elevator in the house to help both him and Genevieve get from floor to floor.

Now, here is where the twist begins. On March 15, 1947, Genevieve Stickney died. According to the death certificate, the cause of death was not suicide but heart disease. The place of death is not the Old Mission Peninsula home but, rather, a Grand Rapids hotel the Stickneys used as their winter residence, the Pantlind Hotel.

For those not familiar with the Pantlind, it was an upscale lodging in the 1930s and 1940s. Today it is known as the Amway Grand Plaza Hotel. The older section is what remains of the Pantlind. Interestingly, it is this section of the hotel that is considered haunted by a former female guest. Could Mrs. Sitckney's spirit possibly be the resident ghost at the Amway Grand? That, however, is another story for another time.

On August 31, 1949, a little more than two years later, Charles died. Bev and I located a copy of Charles' Last Will and Testament and found no mention of a nurse in his estate distribution.

It appeared, from our initial research, the famous "Genevieve Legend" was a complete fabrication. Genevieve died before Charles. She did not hang herself but, rather, died from heart failure at the Pantlind Hotel. There did not appear to be an affair with some nurse, and Charles' estate was distributed to friends and family with small amounts to servants.

We were about to the write the whole legend off as an unsubstantiated myth when another twist occurred. Julie, our Grand Traverse historian, located Charles' final Last Will and Testament. Apparently, the copy we had was out of date.

Charles had revised his will before his death. Guess who was listed as the major beneficiary... *the nurse.* The nurse, in fact, received the majority of Charles' estate that included cars, jewelry, stocks, *and* the Stickney's beloved Bowers Harbor home.

We were in for yet another big surprise. Charles had, in his last year, moved in with the widowed nurse and her children.

Bev and I sat back in disbelief. After all our initial work, we were back to square one. Julie had the phone number of Marilyn, the nurse's daughter. We gave Marilyn a call and, in doing that, discovered the real truth behind the Genevieve Legend.

Kathryn was her name. She had completed her education as a Registered Nurse and worked in a

Marilyn Bassett, Kathryn's daughter

hospital when she met her husband. Upon marriage and beginning a family, she gave up her career.

Marilyn remembers their lives as being absolutely wonderful, a loving family, until the day of her father's unexpected death in 1945. Her mother was suddenly left with unpaid bills, two children, and no income. She returned to nursing and signed up with the local hospital as an in-home/visiting nurse.

It was shortly thereafter that Kathryn became the private nurse of Genevieve and Charles Stickney. Genevieve had a failing heart and Charles was confined to a wheelchair.

Marilyn remembers Mr. and Mrs. Stickney. Mrs. Stickney "ruled the roost" while Mr. Stickney was quiet with a gentle disposition. Both, however, welcomed Kathryn's children to their Pantlind Hotel rooms. The children were even invited to watch the parades that passed just outside their upper floor windows. After Sunday

Photograph courtesy of Marilyn Bassett

Kathryn, the Stickney nurse

Photograph courtesy of Marilyn Bassett

Marilyn, age fourteen, and her brother

school, the sister and brother would walk to the Pantlind where Mr. and Mrs. Stickney would give them money to have a fancy brunch in the hotel restaurant. It was a real treat for the children.

Marilyn suddenly stopped the story. A troubled look crossed her face. We could tell she was contemplating whether or not to tell us something else. She made her decision and continued, "She [Mrs. Stickney] was... *different.*" Marilyn emphasized the word different and recalled something her mother had secretly told her.

Apparently the Stickneys had three adjoining hotel rooms at the Pantlind. Charles had one room and Genevieve the other. The center suite was the nurse's station where the medication and supplies were kept. One day, Kathryn walked into the nurse's station to find Genevieve "tampering" with Charles' medication.

Kathryn immediately became concerned, knowing that mixed medications could be deadly. She feared Genevieve may have been attempting to harm Charles and immediately reported it to their physician, Dr. Whinery. Shortly after that, the doctor came by and removed all the medications, returning with new prescriptions and a locking medicine chest. From then on, the prescriptions were kept under lock and key.

We asked Marilyn if there was some reason why Genevieve would want to harm her husband. Marilyn responded, "I don't know... but I think she really wanted him to go before her."

When we asked why, Marilyn shrugged, "I don't know why. My mother didn't know either."

"Had the couple not been getting along?"

Marilyn responded that there didn't seem to be any problem, "... as far as we knew."

Though Marilyn could not provide the answer, more of the puzzle pieces were falling into place. There is no question that a certain fondness had grown between Kathryn and Charles.

Unknown to others, Charles may have suggested to Genevieve that it would be kind to bequeath their estate to Kathryn. She had treated them with such devoted care and kindness. Adding to that, Kathryn, being a single mother, needed the money (the other members of their family were quite wealthy). Genevieve may not have taken kindly to the idea of giving her beloved Bowers Harbor home to the nurse.

Perhaps in a moment of despair, jealously, and anger, Genevieve had attempted to bring about Charles' death before he could change his will. One can imagine that if an autopsy had been done after Charles' death, a medication overdose would have been blamed on the nurse. This is purely conjecture on our part. However, it does represent a very real possibility.

Marilyn went on to remember Genevieve's death. She was very ill near the end. Her body retained massive fluids from a failing heart. In fact, she retained so much fluid that her limbs swelled to the point where her skin cracked and fluid seeped out. When she went to bed, they would prop her up on huge pillows so she could breathe.

Genevieve died in her bed at the Pantlind Hotel. After the funeral, her body was taken to the Stickney family plot in St. Paul, Minneapolis. Charles couldn't bear the thought of being alone and asked if he could come to stay with Kathryn and the children. Kathryn agreed.

Marilyn let us in on yet another startling revelation. About a year after Genevieve's death, Charles asked Kathryn to marry him. Kathryn declined. She thought of Charles as a dear friend, but she didn't love him in *that* way. Marilyn believes Charles did love Kathryn in a certain way. She believes his proposal was based more on his need to have someone take care of him rather than anything seriously romantic.

Charles in his later years

In June of 1948, while Charles, Kathryn, and her family were at the Bowers Harbor home, Charles changed his will. He bequeathed the majority of his estate to Kathryn and the children.

It was a warm late-August evening in 1949. Charles, Kathryn, and the children were nearing the end of their summer stay at the Bowers Harbor home when Charles suddenly became ill.

They took him from his second floor bedroom down the elevator to the awaiting ambulance. The ride to the first floor was an unusually long and difficult journey that night. Charles looked sadly out through the lattice doors sensing, perhaps, it would be his final moments in the home he and Genevieve had loved. Charles died August 31, 1949 at a Traverse City hospital. Kathryn was by his side.

Kathryn and her family returned to the Bowers Harbor home for the next few summers. The original farmland was later divided and sold.

At the conclusion of our interview, Marilyn added her final comment, her voice dropping a bit, "When we lived there, I remember my mother saying she felt something strange in the house. I never felt anything, but she claims there was something not right there."

When we asked what it was her mother felt, she simply shook her head. "My mother wouldn't say. She just didn't like it." You can listen to our interview with Marilyn in our Web site's Secret Room.

After the interview, we felt a certain sense of resolution. While the Genevieve Legend was wrong, there were certainly elements of truth.

Although there does not appear to be a *romantic* relationship between Charles and Kathryn, there was definitely an affection that existed. It seems possible that Genevieve feared her husband might bequeath their estate to the nurse, Kathryn. She may have even contemplated Charles' early demise to stop him from following through with his plan.

It also seems that the elevator did, in fact, hold the ultimate answer to this mystery. Genevieve did not hang herself there.

Some of Genevieve's personal items

Rather, it was Charles who was the last to look through those lattice doors. On his final journey did he contemplate life's end and regret the mistakes he had made? Perhaps it is his spirit that remains with the elevator.

We can't forget that Kathryn sensed some unusual presence in the home after Charles death. It could be the spirit of Genevieve or Charles who so loved this Bowers Harbor home. And, who knows, maybe Genevieve's spirit cannot rest because Charles gave the home to Kathryn.

We feel satisfied that, finally, the truth behind the Genevieve Legend is known as well as the reasons for its possible haunting. We just had one final question. Why would the Bowery, the oldest part of the property, be paranormally active? Certainly it was not a section of the home to which the Stickney's were particularly attached.

Julie came through for us again. Her further digging into the home's past brought forward the names of the original landowners. They were Chester and Betsey Ann Hartson. The Stickneys had actually purchased the land from one of their daughters in 1909.

Chester and Betsey Ann were among the area's first settlers. The Hartsons, just like the Stickneys, found this scenic area overlooking the bay and fell in love with its beauty. They built the farmhouse, raised a loving family, and together made a living from the land.

In 1898 Betsey became ill and passed away at home. After he lost Betsey Ann, Chester became despondent and sickly. He died in the home just two weeks after his wife. The Bowery is the only remaining part of the original farm. Could the spirits remaining in the Bowery be that of Chester and Betsey Ann?

The true Bowers Harbor Inn story weaves a complex and fascinating tale. Four people from different times and different pasts share one thing in common, a love of this beautiful place on Old Mission Peninsula.

Sometimes the most powerful ghost story is not just about jealousy, hate, and infidelity but of love that remains. This is one of those stories.

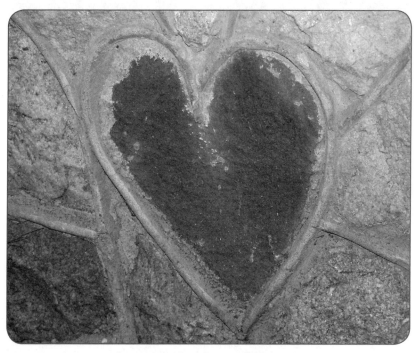

Love is the foundation of the home

Story Ten
The Terrace Inn

Petoskey/Bay View, Michigan
Web site: www.HauntedTravelsMI.com
Secret Room Password: ter99
Paranormal Investigative Teams:
West Michigan Ghost Hunters Society (WMGHS)
and Organization for the Research and Science
of the Paranormal (ORSP)

On a cool, sunny, spring morning, we headed north from Metro Detroit to Petoskey, Michigan to meet Nicole Bray and the WMGHS team. This trip would be to investigate reported paranormal activity at the historic Terrace Inn. We were excited at the opportunity of seeing one of the state's most experienced paranormal groups in action.

After a particularly hectic week, it was good to leave the office for a few days, especially since our destination was this beautiful area of Michigan. In fact, the scenic shoreline of Little Traverse Bay and the numerous boutique shops called to us... *come, enjoy the view and spend some money.* "Work, work, work, but it must be done."

The atmosphere was upbeat. Our favorite tunes were pouring out of the iPod. The first hints of green were sprouting through the still snow-crusted ground. We spotted a few deer, wild turkey, and even a bald eagle along the way. How awesome was this trip! It's great to love your work.

Chatting away, we did not notice that the bright sun and blue sky were about to change. Just ahead, dark storm clouds had formed, perhaps an early sign of what the weekend held in store. When the first large drops of cool rain slammed against the windshield, our conversation quieted. In the distance, rumbles of thunder could be heard. In unison, we looked at each other, smiled, and raised our eyebrows in mock surprise. Perfect!

Following the lakeshore road, we entered Petoskey passing the Gaslight District. This historic area is a must-see for area visitors and has served as a primary shopping district for more than a hundred years. Its streets are lined with period gaslights, unique shops, boutiques, galleries, and fine dining.

Rounding the bend, we turned off US 31 onto a quiet road of Victorian cottages and the Terrace Inn. It would be nice to see Patty and Mo Rave again, the charming owners and managers of the inn.

We met the couple back in 2005 when visiting lodgings for our other book, *Michigan Vacation Guide: Cottages, Chalets, Condos, B&B's.* At that time, they were in the first stages of restoring this historic, forty-two-room inn. Since then, Patty and Mo made significant improvements in restoring the inn's original ambiance. Appreciating the needs of today's guests, however, they added such modern amenities as air conditioning, satellite flat screen TVs, and even a few Jacuzzi suites.

Jacuzzi suite

Stepping into the lobby, we were taken back to a time very reminiscent of the inn's early 1900's construction. Dark wood panels covered the walls with impressive, high ceilings and an ornate staircase. Even the front desk retained its early charm. Of course, the front desk manager didn't look anything like a Victorian lady but a friendly, modern young woman.

Lobby

We asked if Patty and Mo were around. She motioned to the closed dining room doors where the

Standard room

sounds of a commercial grade floor sander could be heard. "Mo's involved right now, and Patty is out," she said. Just at that moment, a poor, masked soul, covered head-to-toe in dust, emerged from the dining room. As it turned out, this dust bandit was none other than Mo. He greeted us with a heartfelt welcome and wished us happy "hunting" before returning to his dusty task.

With suitcase in hand, we arrived at our comfortable rooms styled with period antiques, wallpaper, and bed coverings. The Raves had done a nice job keeping the rooms true to the inn's early Victorian beginning.

That era was a very interesting time in Bay View's history. Since 1875, the little community had fast become one of many popular summer retreats for devout Methodists across the United States. These summer gathering places were known as Chautauqua camps.

For those unfamiliar with the term Chautauqua, it was a religious educational movement in the late nineteenth and early twentieth centuries. These special camps brought religion, entertainment, and culture for the entire community with noted speakers, teachers, musicians, entertainers, and preachers. President Theodore Roosevelt once stated it was "the most American thing in America." Just a few of the noteworthy people coming to Bay View during that period were Helen Keller, Booker T. Washington, and Earnest Hemingway.

Bay View's Chautauqua popularity continued to grow as a result of the community's scenic beauty and proximity to steamboats and railroads. Small Victorian cottages were built to house the increasing number of summer visitors.

One of the Methodists returning each year was William J. Devol, a prominent businessman from Lebanon, Indiana and Treasurer of Bay View's Chautauqua camps. William thoroughly enjoyed spending time in this serene area with his wife, Emma, and three young daughters, Beatrice, Cordelia, and little Virginia. It was here the family shared many memorable summers.

With increasing demand for lodging, Mr. Devol saw the value of a luxury hotel. He took ownership of the old Terrace Inn,

Original Terrace Inn

Photograph courtesy of the Terrace Inn

which had been badly damaged by fire and lay vacant. By 1911, all renovations were completed, and the new Terrace Inn opened its doors. It featured all the latest amenities. A review in the *Petoskey Evening News,* dated July 5, 1911, gave it high praise calling it, "…one of the most complete and convenient structures ever built for hotel purposes."

Nearly one hundred years have passed since that time. Though records have been lost, it seems certain that many distinguished visitors enjoyed the comforts of the inn. Happy memories and joy may have mingled with sadness and tragedy. Whatever happened over the past century, we will never know. However, since the inn's first major renovations in the 1970s, there have been growing accounts of unusual, strange, and perplexing phenomena occurring.

We first heard about the ghostly occurrences from Patty. After purchasing the inn in 2004, they were handed the keys along with the official "ghost" portfolio.

In this well-worn folder were decades of recorded paranormal occurrences experienced by guests. Some of the recurring incidents include visions of a man in a tweed jacket and a woman in a white dress. These apparitions are never seen together but, rather, appear

Photograph courtesy of the Terrace Inn

35 Terrace Inn, Bay View, Mich.

Terrace Inn, circa 1911

to be searching for one another. Other paranormal activity include the hushed whispers of a woman speaking in old-fashioned English, objects moving, and alarm clocks and lights mysteriously turning on.

Of course, this peaked our curiosity. It was time to call in WMGHS to see if they could help find some answers.

Heading up this investigation was the founder of WMGHS, Nicole Bray, and her associate, Robert DuShane, founder of WPARanormal Investigation. Both co-host the Internet radio talk show, WPARanormal. com.

We immediately felt comfortable with these down-to-earth folks. As we chatted, the rest of the crew began to arrive.

Nicole Bray, founder of WMGHS

The group con-
sisted of Julie, Bob,
Aimee, and Jodie.
While all came from
different professional
backgrounds, each
shared a common
interest in ghosts,
hauntings, and the
paranormal. After
introductions, we
told the group of the
reported "hot spots"
of activity based on
our initial interview
with Patty. Nicole
then compared our
info with the report
Patty had completed
a few weeks back.
This information
helps Nicole and her
investigators deter-

Bob and Rob

Nicole, Julie, Aimee, Kat

mine where to set up equipment.

The group broke out, going in different directions, each
member knowing their role. Bob and Rob began the tedious,
time-consuming process of laying cable from the basement to the
third floor. When completed, these cables would connect multiple
cameras to their DVR system located on the second floor.

With all this wiring, we were amazed at how efficiently and
thoroughly they taped down and/or hid cables to ensure everyone's
safety. While this was going on, Aimee and Julie were busy
checking audio and photographic equipment as Nicole went about
gathering EMF (electromagnetic field) levels throughout the inn.
Many paranormal investigators believe that the energy created by
spirits/ghosts can cause unusual spikes in EMF readings.

After everything was set up and ready to go, dinner was next on the agenda. Most of the team had gone upstairs to gather their things when we had our first experience.

It was exactly 7:37 P.M. Bob, Kat, and I were talking in the lobby when Kat noted the back room office light turned on. For a second or two, we stared at the door, expecting someone to come out. No one did and, of course, no one would since the staff had left several hours earlier. We went over to investigate and found the wall switch was flipped to on.

We didn't jump to conclusions. There are a number of natural, logical reasons why lights turn on by themselves. Electrical fluctuations, old wiring, or even high levels of static electricity can cause this event.

We tested the light switch repeatedly. It went on and off as expected. Of course, we weren't able to check the wiring or other electrical abnormalities. The only thing we could do was record the incident in the investigation log.

Soon to be added to the recorded incident list would be the discovery of my laptop sitting on the bed, opened and turned on. I had left the room earlier with the laptop securely stored in my bag. Someone or something had taken it out. There was no way to tell. Check off one more unusual experience.

After dinner, we returned to the inn where Nicole offered some final instructions then broke everyone into two-member teams, assigning us to different floors and locations. Once we all were settled, it was time to "go dark."

Up to this point we found this experience good, light fun. Then the lights were turned off. We were alone in the dark. The thought suddenly struck us that we should have gone with our first idea of a book about the resurgence of impressionistic art in the 1990s. Well, on second thought, maybe not that but anything else that would not require our standing in the dark, in the night, in the quiet.

There is something very unsettling about being alone in the dark, particularly in a strange room. It is totally disorienting and causes the inner child to come out. You're once again waiting for the monster under the bed or in the closet.

Surrounded in silence, you can hear your heart pound and your pulse race as you wait for… something. You're aware of every creak and bump. Shadows are threatening. The first time the lights go out on a ghost hunt will be a memory you'll keep with you a very long time.

Our post for the next hour was the inn's spacious dining room. We had dined here a few years before. It had been a wonderful experience with absolutely delicious cuisine. The dining room's historical country ambiance and great views of the grounds were warm and relaxing.

Things are different now. There are no well-set tables, no happy chatter of people, nor cheerful clinking of glasses and plates. There are no tempting aromas. We are alone in the night, in the quiet, in a big, empty, dusty room with lots and lots of shadows and creaking noises and creepy bumping sounds. We are cowards. How embarrassing. How exciting!

So there we sat with our digital audio recorder, video camcorder, and still camera. We sat and took pictures. We stood up and took pictures. We walked and took pictures. Then we sat some more, and the same damn shadows were everywhere laughing at us.

Dining room, dust not spirit orbs

Our initial apprehension went from excitement to boredom and disappointment. We saw no ghosts and heard no raspy voices from the other side, just darkness and silence.

It was slightly after 11:00 P.M. when we rejoined the others to be given our next assignment. Nicole wondered where Julie and Aimee were. As if on cue, hurried steps echoed down the staircase, and the two missing ladies appeared. It didn't take long for us to realize that something was up. Julie was noticeably shaken, and Aimee appeared concerned.

Julie explained, "We were sitting in room 308 when the alarm just went off. It was blinking 12:15 A.M., which was the wrong time (it was just a little after 11:00 P.M.) When I turned the alarm off, the clock returned to the correct time." Aimee followed by saying they had tested that alarm as well as alarms in other rooms and could not duplicate the event.

We were surprised to hear this, since two years earlier, on our last visit, the alarm in the room directly below this one went off in the same manner. At that time, upon inspection, we noted it was set to off. To turn it off, we had to manually switch the alarm back to on then off.

While this event could have been the result of a natural cause, like electrical fluctuations, for whatever reason an uneasy feeling settled over the group. Anticipation was building after our third unusual experience.

Once everyone settled down a bit, the investigations continued. Returning to the dining room, we now found ourselves accustomed to the creaks and shadows of the old inn, and this room was no longer as unsettling as it had once been.

The clock neared 2:00 A.M. as our next one-hour vigil began. After a long night, we had become a little silly. Doing our best to settle down, we continued our questioning in the hope of eliciting a response from any presence.

Kat began, "Who is the president of the United States?"

I quipped, "Whig or Tory."

"What?"

I repeated, "Whig or Tory."

Kat laughed. Of course, Kat would have laughed at just about anything at this point.

It was then that we both heard an unusual noise from the kitchen, barely audible. The sound was similar to pans lightly brushing against each other.

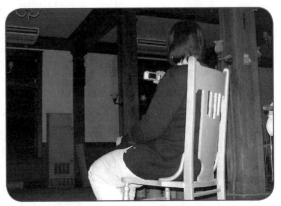

Kat thought she heard a whisper in the dining room

There was also something else. It sounded like a whisper. Silence surrounded us. We said nothing but our glances acknowledged that we had both heard something. In an instant, our senses were alert as uncertainty mixed with excitement.

Being the brave one, I motioned to Kat that I was going into the kitchen to investigate. There were many pots hanging neatly from the walls, but none looked out of place. Moments later I emerged, shrugging my shoulders.

Kat continued to ask questions in the darkness. The brushing metal against metal sound was heard several more times, but no further whispered voices. Then, near the end of the hour, Kat repeated a question she had asked earlier, "Why are you here?"

A few brief moments of silence and then something was heard. Was it another hushed whisper? We couldn't be certain. It was late. We were both exhausted. Perhaps the sound was just our imaginations kicking into overdrive. As we would learn later, our digital recorder would reveal evidence that would lead us to a decidedly different possibility.

So ended the first and very long day of our paranormal investigation of the Terrace Inn. Much too exhausted to think about tomorrow, we went to our respective rooms and were asleep in seconds. Little did we know just how significant the night was or the next evening would prove to be.

We woke up the next morning feeling just a little bit older than we had the day before. The morning was bleak with cold winds and gray skies. Meeting the others in the main lobby over breakfast, with all the equipment still set up and several hours to kill, we decided it was time for a little fun.

Investigations are long and tedious, extending well into the wee hours of the morning. During off-hours, relaxation is important to mentally prepare for the next evening. Relaxation comes in many forms. For our nice little group, that meant heading off to the casino (don't ask) and shopping at some of the area's unique boutiques.

The afternoon was too much fun and ended too soon. It was time, however, to get back to the business at hand. Our light-hearted moods would change as dusk grew near and unexpected events began to unfold.

Patty Rave greeted everyone upon our return. Enthusiastically, she asked how the investigation was going. Nicole indicated that there had been some interesting occurrences the previous night and she was looking forward to this evening's investigation.

Patty went on to explain that shadow figures had recently been seen by the desk manager and cook in the basement's storage and work area. In fact, the cook now refused to go there by herself. This was one area of the inn we had not considered yesterday and would require our special attention this evening.

We went downstairs to review the area before the night's investigation. It was a remote and ominous place where renovations had not taken place.

Mo and Patty Rave,
owners of The Terrace Inn

A long, narrow, dimly lit corridor took you to the dry storage room and work area.

Cracks in the original plaster revealed the wall's skeletal structure with an eerie darkness on the other side. Because of the many restoration projects in progress, a collection of windows, furniture,

Dimly lit basement corridor

and construction materials crowded this already small space.

After our inspection, Rob and Bob began the wiring process. The rest of us took our positions for the night's vigil.

The evening passed with relative calm until 11:30 P.M. Kat and I were stationed on the second floor involved in an EVP session when Nicole appeared. Something had happened in the basement.

As Nicole began to explain what transpired, the sounds of Rob and Bob rapidly ascending the stairs could be heard. They were excited, no doubt about it. Rob disappeared down the hallway without comment while Bob stayed to explain what had occurred.

A light had turned on. Not a significant event by itself since a light had also turned on the night before. However, this time the light had gone on just after an unusual sound had been heard.

This light was in a room not easily accessible. One door was locked while the second entrance heavily blocked with construction materials. The two men entered the room after they removed some of the material. It was completely empty with only a single, pull-string ceiling light burning brightly. Bob also thought they may have recorded an EVP about the same time this had happened. Rob briefly joined the group before returning with Bob to the basement storage room.

Our little group intently watched the video monitor as Rob and Bob repositioned the camera to focus more directly on the area in question. There was no audio. We could only watch them talking as our tension grew. Suddenly, Bob

The monitor was our only link to the activity in the basement

turned his head and walked off camera returning a few seconds later. An animated conversation began with Bob pointing at something off camera.

We could only guess at what was being said. We wanted to join them, but Nicole asked us not to leave the second floor, concerned that we might interfere with their investigation. So, for the next hour we sat in the dark, glued to the small video monitor watching their every move.

When the men finally returned, we were eager to hear what had happened. They, however, were not as eager to share it, saying they needed time to review audio before making any statements. Bob did mention that he thought he'd seen a shadow figure that, unfortunately, had not been caught on video. At that point, Nicole, Rob, and Bob went to another room for their private review and analysis of audio. The rest of us returned to continue our assigned investigation of the upper floors.

At exactly 3:08 A.M., Kat and I were just finishing a rather uneventful period on the second floor when a very excited Nicole appeared.

She breathlessly whispered, "We have a very interactive young male! At least one Class A or B EVP and several Class C."

A Class C EVP means a voice can be heard but is difficult to understand or interpret. Class B means voices are heard, but not everyone will agree on the words. Class A is a voice that can be heard and understood by most people.

A young spirit's disembodied voice was recorded here

Within minutes, everyone came together. Clustering on the large bed in a third floor room, we anxiously peered over Rob's shoulder as he brought up the first EVP on his laptop computer.

Rob indicated that prior to this EVP, he and Bob had been asking if the spirit minded them being

The team gathers for evidence reveal in the early morning hours

there. He then played the audio segment.

At first static, then a faint but understandable voice, "It's time to leave." Excitement instantly spread through the group as Kat and I stood in stunned silence. Even a skeptic would find the voice on the audio difficult to ignore.

The evidence continued to mount. Rob cued up two more EVPs. The next whispered voice was a Class B. "Hurry up" or "I'll be up" were the most likely interpretation. The last EVP captured occurred just before Bob and Rob left the basement. It said, "Come back." Was this ethereal voice trying to tell us something?

It was nearly dawn. Our exhaustion was replaced by a renewed energy as the last EVP was played.

Nicole turned to us saying this was one of the most active investigations she had been on for several years. Excited chatter broke out among the group, which lasted for nearly an hour. Finally, exhaustion returned and with it the reality that we all desperately needed sleep.

We met with Patty and Mo late the next morning and discussed our experiences over the past two nights. They were fascinated by the initial EVPs Rob revealed. Of course, the final analysis couldn't be provided until careful review of the many hours of video, audio, and numerous photographs.

Back in our respective offices, the WMGHS group began their analysis, as did Kat and I. The going was slow and certainly tedious. Coffee breaks were frequent.

Kat and I started on the hundreds of photographs taken, coming across dozens of orb-type images. We immediately discounted these as dust and lens flare in light of the fact that the inn was

Patty and Mo are given the evidence

undergoing massive restoration. Dust was everywhere. It is easy to mistake dust, flying insects, or simple lens flare in photographs as energy orbs.

After going through hours of video, we saw or heard nothing. Finally, we moved on to our audio collection. We were particularly targeting the first evening during our dining room EVP session where we heard noises from the kitchen and thought we heard a whisper. Loading the track into our computer, we quietly sat down to listen.

We asked the first question, "Is anybody here?" To our total surprise, there was an answer, soft and faint, barely audible, "Listen to me." We replayed it again, adjusting sound levels. The words stood out somewhat clearer and appeared to be a female voice. We wondered if we should have listened closer for other signs on that long evening.

Another lengthy series of questions were met with silence. Approximately forty-five or fifty minutes passed.

We asked, "Who is the President?"

There it was. A hushed voice whispered back, "Why should I?"

This EVP was different from the first. Though still quiet, it was clearer and distinctly male. Listen to the actual EVP at our Web site's Secret Room.

Shortly before the end of our session, we repeated a question we had asked before, "Why are you here?" This time the male voice clearly responded, "Abby Sweet."

Could this be the man in the tweed coat looking for his lady in white. Is the lady in white Abby Sweet?

We would need to go back to historical/ancestral records to see what, if anything, we could find. The next week in our office, we spent several days of research scouring the Internet. There we found several records related to an Abigail Sweet including family posts sharing ancestral information with other families.

To complete our research, we headed back to Traverse City and the main district library. One and a half days of scouring microfilm and plenty of coffee added to our growing archives. We also spent considerable time searching online genealogy sites.

Here's what we have been able to assemble. A young girl, Abigail Sweet, is recorded as having come from Ireland to Canada, arriving in America at the turn of the century. She lived in New Hampshire with her family who then moved to New York and later Indiana. Old family letters indicate she became the housekeeper for a prominent Indiana family.

The records are unclear as to how she met her fiancé or who he was, but she was engaged in the early 1900s. We could not, however, find records of a marriage. There is one letter to her family in Ireland, several years later, that indicates she was moving to northern Michigan and expected to take a position as housekeeper for an upscale hotel near a beautiful Michigan lake. That was the last communication we could find from Abigail.

Certainly, based on research and our knowledge of the Devol family, they were considered one of the prominent families in Indiana. Could Abigail have worked as the Devol's housekeeper, later offering her services at the Terrace Inn?

We were never able to locate her fiancé or discover why the marriage did not take place. It's possible he followed her to Michigan. It is equally possible he succumbed to typhoid fever, tuberculosis, or influenza, all epidemics that swept the Grand Traverse area from 1910 through 1920.

WMGHS claimed it had been one of their more active investigations and believed it to be haunted. We completely agreed.

Who or what uttered the soft, eerie words in the basement and dining room may never be known. It added to the mystery of the Terrace Inn haunting, and we had to go back.

A year passed, and the opportunity of visiting the inn presented itself with Ivan Tunney from the Organization for the Research and Science of the Paranormal (ORSP). Ivan was very interested in conducting an investigating. We arranged another visit with Patty and Mo and would meet Ivan and his wife, Linda. Dan Brunner, team sensitive, would also join the group.

We arrived at the inn a little before ORSP and met with Mo. The latest renovations at the inn were impressive. It was obvious Mo and Patty had spent considerable time and money on the changes.

The dining room was completely restored and very appealing. Some of the rooms had been expanded. Fresh paint and period furnishings added to the charm and guest comforts.

Beautifully restored dining room

Perhaps the biggest surprise was down in the basement. A year before, it was rather neglected and used primarily for storage. Now, new walls, ceilings, and rooms transformed the area from creepy to cheerful. They were even adding an old-time ice cream parlor that would be open to the general public.

It was early evening when Ivan and the ORSP team arrived. It was great to see them again. Once they were settled in, everyone was ready to begin. Not wanting to influence Dan and Ivan's impressions, we did not give them historical information on the hotel. They were not given information on the events that occurred with WMGHS.

Dan did his initial walk-through as Ivan took EMF and temperature readings. To our surprise, Dan immediately picked up on all the hot-spots from last year's investigation with Nicole's group.

On the third floor, Ivan and Dan entered Room

Ivan Tunney from OSRP takes EMF readings

308. There was a negative feeling as though they had to get out. Both believed someone jumped out the window, not for suicide purposes but to get to the second floor balcony. Kat and I said nothing but wondered if they were picking up energy from guests trying to escape the hotel fire back in the 1900s, before Devol owned it. This is also the room that Julie, from West Michigan, refused to sleep in because it gave her a "bad feeling."

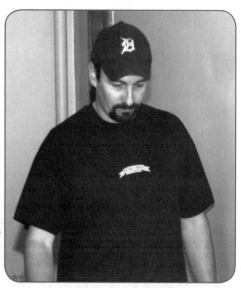

Dan Brunner takes a walk-through

Walking down the hallway, Dan quickly sensed the building had some connection to Baptists or Methodists. This religious connection was also felt in the dining room. It was here, in fact, that Ivan believed sermons and other religious events occurred. At the time, Ivan and Dan were not aware the hotel had once been a noted Chautauqua lodging.

Linda Tunney takes notes

As our travels continued, Dan picked up on the presence of several different energies. One is a man wearing a jacket made of some type of scratchy material, like tweed. The other is a woman in her mid-thirties. He sees this man, in his forties, outside on the balcony. He can't come inside. Dan wasn't sure why. The woman is somehow connected to the man. He also sensed the woman was angry but didn't know why.

We walked into Room 211. Dan stopped for a moment and looked up at us. We had reached the heart of the haunting. This is where the presence of the woman resided. The energy was thick, very strong here. He felt this section of the building would be the most active.

Dan senses Room 211 is the heart of activity

From there, the group moved to the basement. Kat and I wondered if they would encounter the young boy from our previous investigation with Nicole's group.

Dan immediately maneuvered through the new construction into the back storage room. He sensed a young male between the ages of twelve to fourteen years. Dan believed it was the presence of an altar boy or someone who stayed at the hotel for religious reasons. This was the exact area where WMGHS had picked up on an active young male no older than thirteen.

It wasn't long after that things started happening. Kat followed Ivan into the dining room. Last year we had recorded some of our best voice phenomenon in this location. Ivan placed his EMF reader on table and began calling out and praying for the spirits to appear.

The EMF started to buzz. Levels were going up. Kat focused her camera on the meter. It moved to 2.5, which is in the range of paranormal activity. It held for several seconds before dropping back to zero. The EMF levels remained flat until later in the investigation. The second spike occurred around 2:50 A.M. as Ivan again asked the spirits to make themselves known.

Earlier in the evening, Dan and Ivan decided to try an experiment in the basement's storage room. They had pulled a child's stroller from a corner and placed it in the center of the room, hoping the young spirit would move it. Around 2:30 A.M. when Dan, Kat, and I returned, it had not budged. Dan began encouraging the spirit.

EMF levels start to rise in the dining room

"Push that for us. Go, make that move," he said.

Kat focused her camera on the stroller. Seconds passed.

"Did you catch that?" Dan whispered.

"No. What do you see?" Kat responded.

"It's moving," he quietly replied.

Kat repositioned her camera and watched in amazement as the stroller moved backwards, directly toward them. We all stood in silence. It moved more than a foot then stopped. This fascinating video is posted in our Web site Secret Room.

Ivan came down with a laser level to check the floor. It was remarkably level with only a minor dip in front of the stroller. If anything, the slight angle of the floor would have caused the stroller to move forwards not backwards. After the incident, Dan and Ivan moved and repositioned the stroller many times to see if there was some way it might move naturally. It did not.

As dawn neared, Dan returned to the storage room to check the stroller one last time. It had not moved. Sensing the presence was gone, he returned the stroller to its original position against the wall. To do that, he lifted the left, back wheel over a two inch pipe on the floor.

Everyone was in good spirits the next morning, though a little tired. The results from the previous night's investigation were exciting. Over coffee, Ivan and Dan talked about all the noises and music they heard on the third floor. Ivan's wife, Linda, Kat, and I slept like the dead.

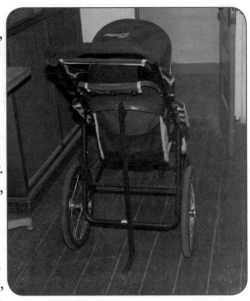

"It's moving," Dan quietly replied

One last time, I thought we should go downstairs and check the stroller. Once there, Linda, Kat, and I couldn't believe what we saw. The stroller had returned to the middle of the floor. How it got there will never be known.

Evidence from both investigations is included in our Secret Room. As of this writing, portions of audio and video are still being analyzed. Once completed, any additional evidence will be available in the Web site's Secret Room.

The Terrace Inn has become a truly lovely bed and breakfast in the beautiful Petoskey area. Mo and Patty have done a fantastic job of restoring this historic hotel. It's a relaxing place to stay even if you're not interested in its ghosts… *and they do have some.* For the ghost hunters out there, stay in the heart of the haunting, Rooms 211 or 308.

About the Authors

Kathleen Tedsen and Beverlee Rydel.

Since 1991, this experienced duo have written and published the Michigan Vacation Guide book series. This book was placed on the Secretary of State's "Read Michigan" list in 1995 and continues to serve as Michigan's most comprehensive publication on unique places to stay in Michigan.

Kat and Bev have been featured on several radio talk shows and PBS TV's "Michigan Magazine." They were also guest speakers at the "Michigan's Haunting Experience" paranormal conference and other public venues.

Since the Michigan Vacation Guide's inception, the authors have traveled thousands of miles across Michigan exploring every region of the state. From the most remote areas of the Upper Peninsula to major urban communities, they have visited many of Michigan's most historical locations.

In their travels, they were surprised at the number of stories they heard from people who had firsthand experience with ghosts and hauntings. Their stories were so captivating it inspired the writers to learn more. Were their encounters just fanciful imaginations, urban legends, or fact?

Kat and Bev went on a journey to find the truth. That is what the *Haunted Travels of Michigan* book is all about. This is their first book in the Haunted Travels series.

Contributors

Special thanks to the following people and organizations. This book could not have been written without their expertise, information and commitment to this project.

Historical Research

Julie Schopieray
Bower's Harbor Inn
The Terrace Inn

Marilyn J. Bassett
Bower's Harbor Inn (Kathryn's Story)

Diana M. Hebner
Sweet Dreams Inn Victorian Bed & Breakfast
John A. Lau Saloon

Jenny Redfern
South Lyon Hotel

Wallace Family Descendants
Sweet Dreams Inn Victorian Bed & Breakfast

Whitney Family Descendants
The Whitney Restaurant

Photographic Forensic Analysis

Angela Clouse
Paranormal Task Force, St. Louis, Missouri

Other Contributions

George Meredith, Meredith Video Productions
"Dinner and a Ghost," Bowers Harbor Inn

Detroit Public Library, Burton Collection

Grand Traverse Public Library

Alpena County Library, Special Collections
Macomb County Historical Society
Macomb County Public Library
Utica Public Library

Reference Source

Grace Whitney Hoff: The Story of An Abundant Life
Author: Carolyn Patch, 1933
(Privately Published)

Paranormal Investigative Teams

Before beginning this book, we spoke with a number of paranormal investigation groups (ghost hunters). Of those we interviewed, there were a few that immediately stood out from the others. These groups demonstrated a true commitment to the field of paranormal investigation. They consistently used sound scientific methods and objective analysis in the collection, review, and identification of paranormal evidence.

Each of these groups conducts investigations under controlled environments to accurately identify suspect paranormal evidence from natural sources. Each actively attempts to debunk/disprove suspect paranormal evidence and is serious in its efforts to help those in distress. None of the groups charge for their services.

We are very pleased to have worked with these reputable teams during the investigation phase of our stories. The names of the team members listed are those who contributed to the investigations in our book. Let us briefly introduce them to you. They are listed in alphabetical order.

Highland Ghost Hunters
Co-founders: Jennifer Marcus and Lisa Mann
Team Members:
Investigator: Keith Carmell
Investigator: Curt Epperly
Investigator: John Ciot
Investigator: Kenny Thorne
Investigator: Chris Jimines
Sensitive/Investigator: Maria DeBard
Formed in October of 2005, Highland Ghost Hunters is led by two dedicated women, Jenny Marcus and Lisa Mann. Adding

to their strength is a core group of experienced investigators and a skilled sensitive. Together they create a friendly, trustworthy team that demonstrates the highest level of respect for individuals and commitment to each case they work.

Highland uses a variety of equipment in their investigations that include infrared video cameras, audio recorders, EMF readers, and temperature gauges. While all members of the Highland team help in equipment setup, Jenny and Lisa take the primary lead in the purchase, maintenance, and setup of equipment.

What impressed us the most with Highland is their dedicated, thorough analysis of audio, video, and photographic material collected during investigations. They also use a very aggressive approach to debunking suspect evidence.

Metro Paranormal Investigations

Co-founders: Chris Forsythe and Wayne Miracle
Team Members:
Tech Manager: Christopher Cloud
Investigator: Wendy Forsythe
Investigator: Deana Miracle
Investigator: Alyssa Miracle
Investigator: Kyle Brown
Investigator: Erin Cloud
Investigator: Timothy Forsythe
Investigator: Russ Gifford
Investigator: Jo Gifford
Investigator: Kevin Johnson
Investigator: Kristie Johnson
Investigator: Doug Milmine
Investigator: Karen Milmine
Investigator/Sensitive: Rita Sacco

Headed by Chris Forsythe and Wayne Miracle, MPI comprises a large group of investigators that brings a diverse collection of skills. From an excellent video technical specialist to dedicated investigators and dynamic psychics/sensitives, MPI has the ability to bring a strong force to each hunt.

In addition to having a large membership, MPI is also one of the best-equipped groups. They maintain a growing arsenal of video and still cameras with specially designed infrared lights, audio recorders, EMFs, and thermo-gauges. In fact, on the technology side, MPI is indeed fortunate to have an expert technical specialist, Chris Cloud. His knowledge of IR and video technology along with his innovative and creative approach to IR and video enhancement allows the team to produce amazingly clear video images in the darkest conditions.

Because of the team's size and equipment strength, they are very capable of handling particularly large investigation sites, as demonstrated by the massive Historic Fort Wayne project. Each investigation is thoroughly planned and thought out by the team's co-founders, Chris and Wayne. Prior to each investigation, teams are given clear instructions with time records precisely maintained.

The team's level of objectivity in analyzing and debunking evidence in order to identify viable paranormal activity is very impressive. This team will go the extra mile to make certain all evidence collected is valid. MPI writes very detailed Evidence Reports. In fact, reports prepared by this group are one of the most comprehensive we've seen.

Michigan's Otherside

Co-Founders: Tom Maat and Amberrose Hammond

Tom Matt (a.k.a. Michigan's Ghost Hunter) and Amberrose Hammond formed Michigan's Otherside in 2007. They are a well-known and extensively networked duo in the paranormal community. The respect they've earned comes from experience, integrity, commitment to research, and evaluation of paranormal phenomena. They're open and sincere in their efforts to support the unity of people involved in the paranormal community.

Tom's experience and interest in the field began more than thirty-five years ago. He has researched and conducted numerous investigations in his continued search for information and understanding about all things related to the paranormal.

Amberrose's fascination with the paranormal began in early childhood. Over the years, Amberrose has worked with several ghost hunting teams around Michigan. Her real passion is researching the history and legends of hauntings.

Tom and Amberrose have the technical and paranormal experience to conduct thorough investigations at smaller locations. Through their vast networks, they can easily call on a variety of trustworthy paranormal teams to join them on larger, more complex sites.

Mid Michigan Paranormal Investigators

Co-founders: Matthew and Melanie Moyer
Team Members:
Investigator: Lee Luke
Investigator: Frank Consolino
Investigator: Julie Consolino

Matthew and Melanie Moyer are the dedicated husband and wife team that lead Mid Michigan Paranormal Investigators. They are both experienced in conducting paranormal investigations and are committed to researching and finding explanations for ghostly phenomena.

During our investigations with Matt and Melanie, we were fascinated by some of the tools they used for investigation. While certainly equipped with high-tech infrared equipment, DVRs, video cameras, audio, EMF, and motion detectors, they also use compasses as a possible identifier of increased energies related to paranormal activity. Use of voice recognition techniques helps them identify the low-level voices of team members from suspect EVPs.

Again, we found this team to be highly analytic and thorough in their evidence collection and analysis.

Organization For The Research And Science Of The Paranormal (ORSP)

Leader: Ivan Ivanovich Tunney
Team Members:
Lead Investigator/Video Technician: Danise Lyon
Sensitive/Investigator: Dan Brunner
Investigator (in-training): Linda Tunney

Originally founded by John Leutz II, the ORSP group is currently led by Ivan Tunney. Ivan is a former medic who is experienced with death and tragedy. Though Ivan does not consider himself to be psychic, he does feel he has some level of sensitivity.

ORSP has a strong commitment to helping people in fear. The group takes every case seriously and will not turn down anyone needing help. The team looks for any natural, physical causes that could be responsible for phenomenon. They will investigate hauntings that may involve demonic spirits and possession. The team uses traditional audio/video equipment as well as EMF, thermo-gauges, and motion detectors.

Ivan's second-in-command and lead investigator is Danise Lyon. Though relatively new to ghost hunting, she has had a long-time interest in the paranormal.

Since early childhood, Dan Brunner has had a special gift. Initially he didn't understand it and was troubled by his ability. Dan eventually sought out a mentor who taught him how to use and control his sensitivity. Dan no longer fears his gift but is eager to discover all that it offers.

Shadow Land Investigators

Co-founders and Lead Investigators:
Charla J. White and Robb Kaczor
Clairvoyant and Psychic Medium: Joan St. John

Shadow Land Investigators is a compact, unique team of two investigators and one clairvoyant/psychic medium. They carry more than thirty years of combined experience in paranormal research and study.

Charla White has been involved in both private and public investigations. Both she and Robb Kaczor have been guest speakers at several conferences, including the Michigan Horror Writers' Club. She focuses on the historical research of each investigation and is a noted specialist at EVP identification.

Robb Kaczor has over five years international investigation experience. In addition to being the group's technical expert, Robb is great with the camera and capturing EVPs.

Joan St. John has worked as a professional clairvoyant and psychic medium for more than twenty years. She has worked with law enforcement agencies in criminal and missing persons cases. Joan currently teaches channeling in the hopes of enabling others to open up safely and ethically to the spirit realm.

Their approach to an investigation is a little different that some. This team relies more on their intuitive nature to identify areas of high paranormal activity and set up their equipment accordingly. They use both a technical, scientific approach as well as a psychic approach during the investigation.

West Michigan Ghost Hunters Society (WMGHS)

Founder: Nicole Bray
Team Members:
Investigator/EVP Specialist: Robert DuShane
Investigator/Infrared Photography Specialist/Technical Director: Brad Donaldson
Investigator: Julie Rathsack
Investigator: Aimee Burnell
Investigator: Bob Webster
Investigator/Public Relations: Jodie Roberts

West Michigan Ghost Hunters Society, headed by Nicole Bray, is a well-established paranormal group formed in the 1990s and based on the west side of Michigan. Nicole's interest in the paranormal began as a young girl of seven or eight. It was shortly after her family moved to a new home that Nicole began experiencing unusual phenomena. It wasn't until many years later that her father revealed the previous owner had committed suicide.

As she grew up, Nicole's fear of ghosts became a fascination that led her to start the West Michigan Ghost Hunters Society. Today, Nicole's core team includes an experienced group of investigators. Brad is the team's expert when it comes to infrared videography and photography. Robert is most adept at EVP analysis. Bob, Julie, Aimee, and Jodie serve as knowledgeable investigators with Jodie also taking on the important role of public relations for the group.

Of course, the West Michigan Ghost Hunters Society also maintains a full arsenal of equipment including DVRs, video cameras, still cameras, EMF, and thermo-gauges. The group works in a well-organized, efficient manner. They are a skilled and knowledgeable team equipped to investigate almost any situation.

Ghost Hunting 101

Ghost hunting is a fascinating field that has evolved into what many people consider a science. The study of paranormal activity is continually improving with an ever expanding cluster of electronic equipment and computers.

Today, most paranormal teams use considerable high-tech tools during an investigation that include such things as video cameras and monitors, still cameras, audio equipment, electronic and temperature gauges, motion sensors, and much more. The technology used is continually increasing and improving. As this evolves, we will be able to explore new dimensions with more accuracy to hopefully clarify many of our mysteries.

Before starting an investigation, some basic equipment is needed. An investigator must have a flashlight since they will often be working in total darkness. There needs to be at least one video camera (infrared lighting is best), still camera, and audio recorder. A handheld camera is nice to have because investigators can take it as they travel to different locations during the hunt. Stationary cameras also have a significant advantage. They are able to capture activity even when no one is around.

When a request is received for an investigation, normally the first thing that happens is to interview the people making the request. It's important to develop an understanding of the parties involved, their concerns, and the paranormal activity.

Often an investigator will ask rather personal questions of people claiming a haunting to determine authenticity. These questions will frequently cover topics such as medical and mental history, drug use, and religion. If there is something going on that could affect their judgment, you may want to reconsider the investigation. Since paranormal groups rarely charge a fee, there is no reason to spend time or risk your safety on these types of alleged hauntings.

Just as important is the history of the people and events involved that may be part of the haunting. What happened in the past may be directly related to what is happening now. Many times an investigator can spend hours if not days on research in libraries, on the Internet, and in personal interviews with local historians or relatives of the deceased. This is a tedious yet critical part of any search.

There are several different techniques used by the groups we have worked with and also some similarities. Every team is different.

There really is no right or wrong way to handle an investigation. Some teams use a skeptical approach going in and attempt to debunk (disprove) activity. Other investigators use a more open approach. Additionally, there are teams that never use a sensitive, some groups will bring in a sensitive or psychic on occasion, while others use them as a regular and critical part of their investigation.

Many paranormal groups use a pared approach on an investigation. The leaders will break their members into teams of at least two people. This is done for several reasons.

First and foremost, safety is a primary concern. On an investigation, normally lights are turned off in the building. If outdoors, they are conducted at night. One person alone could trip in the dark or become overly frightened and have no one there for support.

Another important reason is to verify a personal experience. A personal experience is something not captured on video or audio, but something that you feel, sense, or see. In the dark, an individual's imagination can play tricks. However, if two people see, hear, or feel something, then it is much more likely to have occurred.

Documentation is critical on a hunt. Mark down exact times and locations as the team progresses and if any actual activity happens. It's important to know where team members are each step of the way. All too often, an EVP or apparition turns out to be a member of the group. During an audio session, make certain no one whispers or they will suddenly sound like an EVP when examining audio later.

As our interests in ghost investigation grew, we realized there were many terms and equipment used in the paranormal community. We were not completely familiar with or did not fully understand all of their meanings. Our readers will range from very experienced to very inexperienced.

To help those of you not completely familiar with all the words and equipment used in the realm of ghost hunting, we have complied a glossary. The words listed below are some of the more common terms and definitions used in the industry of paranormal investigation.

This glossary will provide you with many of today's definitions and often include our interpretations. Our glossary is not meant to be all-inclusive but rather to provide the reader with some of the more fundamental words and definitions used.

Apparition

A spirit or energy that is visible to the human eye and can be captured on video or in a photograph. Generally, it has the shape resembling a human form, but it may take the shape of an animal.

Astral Plane

A level of existence referred to by some philosophies and religions, besides the normal physical world that we live in. It is the first metaphysical plane beyond the physical. The term has been used for centuries. Many believe that spirits and apparitions come from this plane.

Automatic Writing

A means for mediums and sometimes ordinary people to transmit communication from the spirits. Many believe the spirits are actually communicating with us through the writing either by directing the hand of the writer or by going through the writer's mind.

Channeling

Two types of channeling exist. In the first, a sensitive or psychic will speak to the spirits. The second form is when the person goes into a trance. They actually leave their bodies and are possessed by the spirit. Often times, this person will become very rigid and their voice may change. The spirit will then answer questions from the group.

Clairvoyant

A person who learns information about a person, place, or thing not normally known by the average person. This is a form of extra-sensory perception. These people can often perceive what has happened in the past or will happen in the future.

Cleansing Prayer

A prayer to cleanse any negative or residual energy that may attempt to attach itself to people during paranormal investigations. It is also the spiritual cleansing of a home to eliminate psychic disturbances or negative energies.

Cold Spot

A localized area where the temperature is noticeably colder. Often this occurs as a sudden temperature drop. It is considered the result of spirits or spirit energy using the heat to manifest or produce some other type of activity.

Demonic Spirits

These are supernatural and evil spirits that are frequently hard to control. Often they are referred to as fallen angels. Frequently, they surface during the use of a Ouija Board.

Direct Voice

A voice that is paranormally produced, often by a medium. The voice is frequently heard during a séance. Often it is the result of poltergeist activity.

Divining Rod

Traditionally, two brass "L" shaped rods that investigators hold in their hands. The rods are used to detect high levels of energy or spirit activity. When the rods cross, energy is high. Brass is used to prevent interference due to the Earth's magnetic field.

Ectoplasm

A white-gray transparent substance often resembling a mist. It may materialize as a result of spiritual energy or psychic phenomenon.

Electronic Voice Phenomenon (EVP)

The voices, of spirits or ghosts, speaking words at a decibel level too low for people to hear but often recorded on audio recorders. Generally, they are soft, almost like a whisper, and frequently sound raspy.

Electro Magnetic Field (EMF)

An area with high levels of electronically charged objects, an EMF is often the result of energy from a spirit or ghost. It may also be the result of electrical wiring or machinery.

Entity

Used to refer to a spirit or ghost. It has a distinct existence but may not have a material form or body.

Exorcism

The practice of removing demons or evil spirits from the body of a person who has been possessed. It is often done by an exorcist, frequently clergy, involving prayer and religious acts. The person possessed is not considered evil, and the exorcism is looked at as a cure. During an exorcism, the person being cured can become extremely violent.

Extra Sensory Perception (ESP)

A person's ability to retrieve information using paranormal means and not physical senses. Often people with ESP are thought to have psychic ability to include telepathy, precognition, and a six sense.

Fairy

Generally these are small creatures, from the dead, with human form and having magical powers. In the U.S. they are considered good luck, but in Europe fairies are evil creatures known for casting bad spells.

Fear Cage

An area in a room with extremely high EMF readings from excessive electrical wiring or equipment. Many people have strong adverse reactions when in a fear cage too long and often think they are experiencing paranormal activity. Physical effects can include nausea, headaches, skin rashes, and hallucinations.

Ghost

The image of dead people, often looking very much like themselves in appearance. Ghosts are most often seen in places they used to live or visit regularly, such as a loved one's home. They can also attach themselves to a possession they once owned. Frequently, they are responsible for paranormal activity to include cold spots, objects moving, apparitions, and footsteps. These spirits can be both good and bad.

Haunting

A place, person, or object that has repeated paranormal activity. These activities would include sightings of apparitions, voices, objects moving, strange sounds, and bad/sad/eerie personal feelings.

Indirect Voice

The voice of a spirit that is heard through a conduit such as a sensitive or medium.

Infrared Light

A light source that goes beyond normal light waves to illuminate in the dark.

Infrared Thermometer

Used to measure the temperature of an object from a distance. Often they are called laser thermometers because a laser is used in aiming.

Intelligent Haunting

When a spirit or ghost is aware of its surroundings. Often they will respond to questions being asked or make noises such as footsteps, turn lights on, and close doors. In an intelligent haunting, it is not uncommon for objects to move or be hidden. The spirit can take on traits of the living person with certain odors or smells from perfume, flowers, cigarettes, etc.

K-2 Meter

A new and supposedly advanced EMF detector that uses lights instead of a needle to detect energy levels. It can be used to communicate with the spirits by asking them to flash the light for yes/no answers.

Matrixing

A person's ability to see something familiar, most often in a photograph, from a series of complex colors or designs. The most common objects seen are a face or body. Extreme caution should be used when reviewing photographs that are dark or blurred to avoid this.

Medium

A person with the ability to communicate with the dead. Physical mediums draw energies so their clients will hear or see images and sounds. Mental mediums will see, hear, and sense the sounds. The spirit communicates through the medium.

Orb

A circular, translucent, light-colored floating object that represents a source of energy. When a lot of orbs are seen, it can mean the manifestation of a spirit. They are very rare. Generally, what many consider orbs are simply dust, bugs, pollen, and other small articles suspended in the air. When the small object gets close to a camera lens, it can appear large and translucent. Caution should be used when considering an orb as authentic.

Ouija Board

A flat surface with letters, numbers, and symbols used to communicate with the dead. Normally, participants place their fingers on a movable object in the center of the board, a planchette, which is moved across the surface of the board and reveals responses to participants' questions. Many believe they are dangerous and should be avoided. It is easy to release evil spirits or demons and become spiritually possessed.

Paranormal

A term used to describe something out of the ordinary that cannot be readily explained. The word itself does not necessarily mean something, someone, or someplace is haunted.

Parapsychologist

A person who studies the paranormal, such as survival of a spirit after death. They use a variety of methodology and testing in their work including laboratory research and fieldwork.

Photographic Cameras

Instruments used to capture an image. The most common instruments are 35 millimeter and digital cameras. Some paranormal groups prefer 35 millimeter cameras since there is a negative image on film that cannot be tampered with. However, more and more investigators are reverting to digital cameras because of the reduced expense in buying and developing film in addition to the improved quality of the photograph.

Poltergeist

A spirit or ghost that actively moves objects. A few even speak and have distinct personalities. Generally, they occur around a person and are thought to come into existence when the spirit experiences unusual rage or very strong emotion at the time of their death.

Psychic

A person with the ability to sense things that the average person cannot. This person is said to have extra-sensory perception. People with psychic abilities are often referred to as mediums or sensitives.

Residual Haunting

A haunting that is replayed in which there is no intelligent spirit or ghost. They are simply repeating some event, usually very traumatic or emotional, over and over again. It is similar to watching a movie again and again. The same activities occur with little change.

Séance

When a group of people gathers in an attempt to communicate with the dead. Often the séance is led by a medium. This person acts as the go-between for the living and the dead, relaying questions and responding with answers.

Spirit

Very similar to a ghost. The two words are often interchangeable. It is simply the thoughts and feelings of a person who has died. As with ghosts, spirits can be good and bad.

Supernatural

Very similar in meaning to paranormal, but more directly related to the spiritual world. It refers to events, people, and activities that cannot be explained using traditional concepts. Most notably, a term used for actions pertaining to spirits or ghosts.

Thermal-Imaging Digital Camera

A camera that records images that the traditional camera cannot see. Primarily, images are recorded based on the amount of heat given off by the subject. It relies on infrared readings and works in darkness, fog, or smoke.

Voice Phenomenon (VP)

Very similar to an Electronic Voice Phenomenon except it can be heard with the ear. To listen to a Voice Phenomenon, audio recorders are not needed. The voices of spirits or ghosts are speaking at a decibel level high enough for the average person to hear.

Vortex

A spinning or whirling event that can be captured on film. It is usually translucent and resembles a small tornado. Many believe it acts as a portal for spirits to come and go.

White Noise

The background hiss or static that is heard on a video recorder. Many times, the white noise has to be filtered out in order to hear an EVP.

Locations

We would like to thank the managers, owners, and innkeepers of the following locations for their cooperation and patience during our visits. While you are traveling through Michigan, these locations are a must see.

Story One

The Whitney Restaurant
www.thewhitney.com
4421 Woodward Avenue • Detroit, MI 48201
(313) 832-5700

Whether it's a snowy night in the depth of winter, a sizzling evening in the height of summer, or a crystal clear midday Sunday, there's nowhere to enjoy relaxed fine dining quite like at The Whitney, Detroit's grandest, most elegant restaurant. Housed in a 115-year-old, 52-room mansion with delicate, ornate wood carvings, Tiffany stained glass windows worthy of a cathedral, and topped by Detroit's coolest lounge, the third floor Wintergarden, The Whitney offers meals to savor and visits to remember.

Story Two

Detroit Historic Fort Wayne
www.historicfortwaynecoalition.com
www.detroithistorical.org
6325 West Jefferson Avenue • Detroit, MI 48209
(313) 833-1805

Throughout its more than 160-year history, Historic Fort Wayne has largely been peaceful, serving as an infantry garrison and a primary induction point for Michigan troops from the Civil War through the Vietnam War. The Fort is currently owned and operated by the City of Detroit. Every summer, the City's Department of Parks and Recreation hosts historic re-enactments, special events, and outdoor activities for visitors.

The Historic Fort Wayne Coalition group of re-enactors is a major support team for the Fort. Beyond their involvement in the re-enactment events at the Fort, they are required, as members, to volunteer hundreds of hours each year to the site where they do their re-enacting. Donations towards their restoration efforts are always appreciated.

Story Three

The Locker Room Saloon
www.lockerroomsaloonlive.com
7790 Auburn Road • Utica, MI 48317
(586) 731-3362

The first and only audience participation bar in Michigan! No dress code and no velvet rope. When you come, be prepared to take part in the craziest bar experience you've ever had. Their focus is placed on their customers by providing a unique house party atmosphere. This includes, but is not limited to, dancing on the bar, playing your sticks, singing, and just being loud. They'll even let you behind the bar.

Story Four

Sweet Dreams Inn Victorian Bed & Breakfast
www.myspace.com/sweetdreamsinn
9695 Cedar Street (Off M-25) • Bay Port, MI 48720
(989) 656-9952

With a breathtaking view of the Saginaw Bay, The Sweet Dreams Inn Victorian Bed & Breakfast is a welcome and peaceful respite from a hurried world. Surrounded by stately trees and in a quiet residential area, the elegantly restored turn-of-the-century mansion sits on four-and-a-half acres. The country furnishings help to create a setting of quiet, peaceful splendor amidst spacious rooms of rich wood paneling, oak and wood plank flooring. A second floor sunroom is furnished with wicker furniture, books, and other memorabilia from an enchanted past. Enjoy your stay in one of its seven rooms.

Story Five

The Indigo Inn and Down and Under Lounge and Grille
www.theindigoinn.com
12 South Division Avenue • Fremont, MI 49412
(231) 928-1240

Built in 1923, this historical hotel was originally designed as, and remains, a homey and welcoming place for guests, much like an old English tavern and inn. The inn offers everything you need for a relaxing night away from home. For some laughs and a good time, the Down &

Under Bar & Grille has a fun and casual atmosphere. As part of your overnight stay, enjoy breakfast in their café by choosing from the menu. Stay for two nights, and a light supper of assorted appetizers is included. Browse the Gallery & Gift Shop, then walk the friendly streets of Fremont and visit the unique stores in the historical downtown.

Story Six

John A. Lau Saloon
414 North 2nd Avenue • Alpena, MI 49707
(989) 354-6898

Welcome to Alpena's oldest historic saloon. It serves full lunch and dinner menus. Voted number one "beef restaurant," their steaks are something to try. Don't forget to check out their micro brews, including their own special Lau's Bootleg Brew. In 1987 the saloon was completely renovated to reflect an atmosphere reminiscent of the 1800s.

Story Seven

Cadieux Café
www.cadieuxcafe.com
4300 Cadieux Road • Detroit, MI 48224
(313) 882-8560

Featherbowling, steamed mussels, more than a dozen beers from Belgium... at the Cadieux Café, as the bumper sticker on the wall says, "It's Beautiful To Be Belgian." Since its days as a Prohibition-era speakeasy, the Cadieux Café has been a social hub for metro Detroit's Belgian population. The Michigan Traditional Arts Program awarded the Cadieux Café the Michigan Heritage Award for "continuing family and community cultural traditions with excellence and authenticity." Live music also attracts the twenty-one to thirty-five year-old crowd. It's still beautiful to be Belgian at the Cadieux Café, but you're more than welcome to pretend.

Story Eight

South Lyon Hotel
www.southlyonhotel.com
201 North Lafayette Street • South Lyon, MI 48178
(248) 437-7516

Located in downtown South Lyon, this historical landmark has been in operation for over 137 years! Offering the best food, entertainment and featured events, the South Lyon Hotel also provides banquet facilities in The Oak Room. Something is always happening here! They have daily lunch specials, nightly dinner and drink specials, two TEN-FOOT big screen TV's for your favorite sporting events, and Happy Hour every day until 5:00 P.M.

Story Nine

Bowers Harbor Inn Restaurant
www.bowersharborinn.net
13512 Peninsula Drive • Traverse City, MI 49686
(231) 223-4222

Built in the 1880s and remodeled in the 1920s as a summer retreat for Chicago lumber baron J. W. Stickney and his wife Genevieve, Bowers Harbor Inn sits peacefully along West Grand Traverse Bay amidst the majestic oaks and pines of Old Mission Peninsula. It is a legendary home of elegant dining. Situated on Grand Traverse Bay, Bowers features the famous smoked whitefish dip, fish in a bag, morel crusted scallops, and more. Enjoy casual dining at The Bowery, an Old Mission Original, with its famous BBQ ribs and lake perch. Over the years, these restaurants have received numerous awards for their cuisine, service, and ambiance.

Story Ten

The Terrace Inn
www.theterraceinn.com
1549 Glendale Avenue • P.O. Box 266 • Petoskey, MI 49770
(800) 530-9898

Well, it's been almost a hundred years, and plenty of things have changed! But don't worry, the unique character of the inn remains intact, complete with a fireplace-graced lobby, odd-shaped closets, and wide verandas. Nostalgic guests love rocking in the same chairs as guests did in 1911. Cottage rooms remain TV-free and are the most original. Their newly created suites beckon the more adventurous vacationer and include a whirlpool tub, fireplace, cable, plus a kitchenette. The inn has an excellent dinning room with a 1950's style ice cream parlor coming soon. It looks forward to a State Historic Designation soon!